I NEED A BAWSS IN
MY LIFE

By

Rae Zellous

Table of Contents

ALL MONEY AIN'T GOOD MONEY

Thursday April 13, 2014

"Fuck me...Fuck me...Harder, daddy...Harder, daddy!" Sexy Duvall, screamed seductive profanities that echoed off of the walls of the *Double Tree Hotel* at one of her tricks, even though she wasn't feeling a thing. Her John's dick was small, but his money was long. His baby-sized penis throbbed, covered in her pussy juice. He was sweating hard trying to get his nut. He concentrated as Sexy instructed him, trying to save time. "Come on, baby, Cum...Cum, baby!" All she wanted was the money.

Her client was Bradshaw Hemsley, an Allegheny County Defense Lawyer for the city of Pittsburgh. He had fought a case for her in 2011 and won. She had rewarded him with a shot of head and he had been turned out ever since.

Going down on her, Bradshaw, placed Sexy's legs on his shoulders. Her pussy hairs were shaven clean, her clit protruded, hard and visible. It poked out, Bradshaw twirled circles around it with his tongue. Her pussy lips hung a little as they covered his mouth his tongue stabbed in-and-out of her pussy hole.

"YOU MUTHAFUCKA...EW, YOU MUTHAFUCKA! Make mommy cum... Make mommy cum!" The least Bradshaw could do was make her cum, Sexy thought, palming his head, force-feeding him her dripping snatch. She wanted to have an orgasm, but she knew in order for her to get paid she would have to make him cum also. "Ooooh, shit...Shit...Shit! I'm cumin', Brad, I'm cah-cah-cuuum-minnn!"

Grabbing Bradshaw by the sides of his face, Sexy removed his face from her pussy. "Fuck my mouth, daddy. I wanna taste my pussy on ya dick. I wanna taste ya nut. Explode ya load in this hot, wet mouth of mine. I wanna swallow for you, daaad-Ay!"

Climbing aboard Sexy's face, Bradshaw, guided his dick through Sexy's succulent lips, and slid his small man-part in-and-out of her mouth. His balls slapped off of her chin again and again. Sexy's medium size hands gripped his ass cheeks, her right hand middle finger wiggled its way into his asshole.

"Yeeaah, do that...Do that, Sexy!" Bradshaw begged as Sexy's manicured finger fingered his asshole while her other hand clawed into the meat of his buttock. Bradshaw's freak ass loved it. The faster he pumped and fucked her mouth, the more he moaned, and his asshole clinched tightly around her finger. Sexy knew that Bradshaw was about to cum.

"Oh shit! Oh shit...I'm cummin', Sexy. Baby, I'm cummin'!" Brad, exhaustingly said, pumping and thrusting his hips filling Sexy's mouth up with all his dick had to offer. The creamy, white cum shot into the walls of Sexy's mouth. She gulped and gulped, swallowing every bit of it.

"Mmmm, daddy. That was so good, thick, and delicious," Sexy said, wiping her face, and licking her finger.

"Ah...ah, damn you," Brad said after rolling over onto his back. "Oh...Oooh, that was great!" He told Sexy.

Gathering her clothing, she headed to the bathroom, where you could hear her cleaning herself and rinsing her mouth out. She gargled and spit mouthwash into the toilet before flushing it. "SWOOSSH!"

Sexy Duvall, was a thirty-five-year-old stripper and reality TV star. She gained television popularity starring on VH1's reality television show *Love & Trap Muzik, Pittsburgh,* opposite of a local rapper named DQ-Dawg who was an up-and-coming artist that had shot to the top of the charts with his single, She *Like It From Da Baaack!* On screen they played a troubled couple striving for success. They were to start shooting for the second season in June, but until then Sexy was still stripping and tricking in order to pay her bills.

As a good business woman, Sexy, negotiated a deal that allowed her twenty-year-old daughter, America Duvall, to star on a few episodes and managed to cause enough controversy to win her a small following.

Thanks to her face on the show, Sexy rose to ghetto-stardom. Before the show, she made several thousand a week. Now she was Pittsburgh's highest paid stripper and was being called to host parties nationally. So now she averaged several thousand a night. Plus, she was selling pussy after her shows, and due to her new found success men and women were willing to pay whatever her asking price was.

Walking out of the bathroom she gazed at Bradshaw as he stood with her money in his hand. "Same time next week?" He asked.

"If I don't have any parties to host. I'll let you know early on in the week," she told him.

"But one day next week, right?" Bradshaw couldn't go a week without her.

"Yesss, daddy."

"Here you go, doll." The older, white, bald man, Bradshow Hemsley, said handing Sexy Duvall two-thousand dollars.

"Thank you, Bradshaw." She moved towards him for a kiss on the cheek, adjusted her spandex dress, and walked in her stilettos out the hotel door.

Inside of the hotel parking lot her *Aston Martin Vanquish* waited. "Yes, I'm on my way..." she purred into the phone to another one of her tricks, auto-starting her car.

***

It was five A.M. on a Friday, by the time Sexy finished with her third and final client. Physically exhausted, she couldn't wait to get home, take a shower, and get in her own bed.

Rolling through the city of Pittsburgh, her high end rimmed wheels flickered water as they rotated. Rain was deflected by her windshield wipers as she looked out of it onto the road ahead. While see was earning her money from her last trick, a light rain had begun to fall. Which caused yellow, blinking, traffic lights to reflect off of the wet streets as her metal horse galloped on the way to her palace.

The night had been good to her, and the pay was even better. She had came at least six times, and earned close to ten-thousand dollars.

The following week she was being flown to New York by TV producers. She also was supposed to hook up with a record executive. Life couldn't be better.

Looking down at her cell as it rung a melody, and glowed off-and-on, she picked it up, and examined the number of the caller.

"Who da fuck is this?" She asked herself. Pressing a button on the side of her phone, she caused it to stop ringing, then made a quick decision to answer it, "Sexy Duvall," she answered.

"Hey Sexy...This is her, yo!" She heard the caller say to someone.

"Can I help you?" Sexy asked, wondering how the caller got her number. She hoped it was not a groupie calling her business line. She had already changed her number twice because of that.

"It's the dude you gave ya card to at *Reflections*." Reflections was a strip club owned by Sexy Duvall's manager, Dominican Flames, and it was where she worked. She did give her cards to potential clients, but she could not put a face to this particular caller. "I'm on my way home," she told him.

"Aw, don't go home. Come fuck wit' me. I'll make it worth ya wild," the caller said and paused.

"If I turn my car around you better make it worth my wild." Sexy told him.

"I gotta stack fo' me and my man to hit," the caller said and paused again waiting for a response.

"Bye! You wasting my time..."

"...Hol' up! Fifteen?" The caller negotiated.

"Twenty-five," Sexy replied.

The caller conversed with his man as Sexy listened.

"Cool, aight." She heard two men talking, "Aight. We got you. Where you wanna meet?"

"Meet me at *Reflections*, I'm close to there now."

"We are too." They agreed to meet at *Reflections* nightclub, it had closed at two A.M. on this particular night so they would have to meet in the parking lot.

Eight minutes later, Sexy watched as a car pulled into *Reflection's* parking lot, its headlights lit up her face as it pulled in, and parked horizontally in front of her car.

"What the fuck?!" Was all that Sexy could say as she watched two armed men exit their car and approach hers with their weapons drawn.

Fumbling through her purse, her hand searched for her .380.

Seeing Sexy rambling through her purse, one of the masked men let three rounds go, "POP-POP-POP! Fuck bitch!" Three rounds filled Sexy's body. The last shot blew several locks of her micro-braids off, tearing pieces of her flesh and skull off with her weave.

"YO! NIGGA, WHAT DA FUCK?!" The other masked man shouted. "We 'pose to be robbin' da bitch, not killin' her!"

Sexy laid slumped to the side, her body was left stretched over the arm-rest to the passenger side. Blood leaked through the bullet holes that burned through her thin dress.

"CRASH!" The masked man that shot her used the butt of his Glock and busted the driver-side window. The glass shattered onto the ground and Sexy's stiff body.

"Nigga, shut da fuck up," the shooter said, unlocking Sexy's car doors. "Pop da trunk," he told the other assailant.

When the shooter opened Sexy's car door, she let off two shots. Bullets blasted through the shooter's mask and chest, striking him with two deadly blows; once in his pecks and once in the forehead. The impact from Sexy's shots forced his body backwards. "POP!" He released one final shot before stumbling backwards, and collapsing to his demise.

Uncertain of what had just transpired, the other jack boy panicked, and ran for his car. But as he tried to pull away, Sexy pulled her shift into drive. "VRRRRNN, BOOM!" She crashed into the side of the rear-end of the robber's car, and made him fishtail as he fled from the scene.

"SKURRT!" Sexy's foot abruptly stopped her car. She managed to put it into park. "Fuck...Ah...Ah...Ah," gasping for her breath as the bullet holes in her body leaked more and more bodily fluid.

Using all of her strength, she reached for her cell phone. In pain, she managed to emergency call 9-1-1, "Helll-helllp," was the final word she got out before she passed out.

**

After receiving the news about her mother being shot, America Duvall, Sexy Duvall's twenty-year-old daughter, collapsed and screamed. The second call she received hurt her even more, the news about her mother had caused her grandmother to have a massive heart attack.

Now she had to deal with two very close family members at death's door. She couldn't gather herself. America screamed and screamed. Her cell phone rung repeatedly as she screened the calls and only answered for the creator of *Love & Trap Muzik, Pittsburgh*, her aunt, and her brother, Renault "Ren" Duvall.

Pacing back and forth, she grew impatient as she waited for Ren to come take her to the hospital. "What am I gonna do without 'em...What am I gon' do?" She questioned herself, feeling confused.

Then her cell phone rung, it was her brother Ren.

"Yea, I'm on my way out, brother."

LET DOWNS & COME UPS

"What the fuck you mean you don't have the footage?! What the fuck do you mean you gave the footage to the police, ma'fucka?! I got TMZ calling me asking for it. They try'na give me ah hunid bands fo' it, and you just gave that shit away!" Dominican Flames yelled at the head of her security, inside of her office at *Reflections*. She was on her way back from Philly when the shooting occurred. She called a meeting with her security team and goons as soon as she got back to Pittsburgh. She flipped after hearing that the head of her security team gave the valuable footage of Sexy Duvall's shooting to the police. The incident had taken place in the parking lot of her club, *Reflections*.

"I didn't know," the security guard tried to defend his actions.

"You didn't know?! What?! Are you stupid?! Huh, ma'fucka?! Are you stupid?! Man, get the fuck out my face...Get the fuck out my face!"

"Come on, Dom." The security guard pleaded for reason.

"Get the fuck outta my face! Go find som'in' to do while I figure shit out. I'll call ya ass when I'm ready fo' ya ass to come back. No! Matter of fact, go get that nigga's blood off my parking lot. That's what ya ass can do. Yea, go do that, and think about that dumb ass shit you did."

"Dom, they said it was for an investigation." The security guard held his ground.

"I don't give ah fuck! You don't release shit to anybody unless you get my permission. Did they have ah warrant?" Dominican Flames asked.

"No."

"Mm mm mm, you's ah stupid ma'fucka. You better get outta here 'fo' we have ah real problem up in here, seriously." She told him, standing amongst her security and goons, getting angrier and angrier. What she didn't know was the security guard had also sold two copies of the footage to the Duvall family.

***

The next day around nine A.M., DQ Dawg was talking to his man, 2 Gatz, "Shit's crazy, Earn'. I couldn't sleep ah wink last night, not ah minute, not ah second, dawg. I tossed and turned, an' shit thinkin' 'bout my bitch gettin' hit." DQ Dawg was speaking about Sexy Duvall. "But they said she shot back, and killed one of dem boys, though."

"Hell yea. She's ah G fo' that, she's gangsta as hell.

DQ Dawg's cell phone vibrated. Picking it up, he screened the caller. "This them people from the show...Yo!" He answered his phone, "Okay...Okay...Cool."

2 Gatz listened to one side of DQ Dawgs' conversation. "We start shooting *Love & Trap Muzik* Monday. They want me to tell everybody following me on social media to check out *Love & Trap Muzik's* website Tuesday night at eight P.M., they gon' advertise the new season. Plus, tonight they want me to post ah condolence drop on their site." DQ Dawg told his man.

"That shit is crazy. Sexy, her mother dropping dead after hearing about her getting hit up. Shit's crazy." 2 Gatz said.

"Hell yea, that shit's the craziest." DQ Dawg replied.

"So what you got planned fo' the show?" 2 Gatz asked.

"I'ma just do me, you know? I got some shows and you know, the new CD and book I'm droppin' and whatever the show got planned. I know they gon' try to put me in a spot with that bitch ass nigga, Block N Bricks." DQ Dawg and Blocks N Bricks were rap rivals.

"Hell yea. You know they gon' throw in that drama." 2 Gatz added.

"If they do that shit, that's just what they go get some drama." DQ Dawg and Blocks and Bricks were once rap partners now they battle for rap supremacy.

***

"Who's pussy is this...Who's pussy is this?!"

"Blocks N Bricks...Blocks N Bricks...Blocks N Bricks." Blocks N Bricks was beating some pussy up at 9:05 A.M., it sounded like he was laying one of his tracks. The groans and moans of the morning sex session were rhythmic.

Feeling as if he was about to cum, he pulled out. "OHHH...Ah...Ah."

"Why you pull out? Fuck!" The T.H.O.T asked. "I was about to cum." She said.

Then Blocks N Bricks maneuvered his body on top of hers, lying in the 69 position. With his dick in her face, he tongued her pussy, and waited for her to put his dick in her warm, wet mouth. He flicked his tongue back and forth, up and down her clit. She loved the way he was tonguing her pussy. He spit, licked, and smothered his face in her close-cut beaver as he humped his hips pounding her cocksucker with hard, thick dick. What he was doing to her cunt drove her crazy.

She yelled in ecstasy. "Aaaah, Block...Block...Ooooh, ew..."

"...Eat that dick, bitch! You nasty bitch. Ain't you my freak bitch, huh...Huh?!" Blocks N Bricks pulled his head back from her pussy to ask her.

"Yes! Yes! Mm hm, yes!" She answered, barely able to talk.

Ring! Ring!

"Don't answer it." The T.H.O.T told Blocks N Bricks, hearing his phone ring and vibrate.

***

"That's the footage?" Monte Bucks asked, gazing at America's cell phone.

"Yep." America answered.

"Let me see the footage." Monte Bucks said, reaching for the phone. America didn't stop him.

"Like I said, that's one copy. The short version. I have the full version for you too. But them fuck boys got ah third copy. So if you wanna capitalize off of this opportunity, as you call it, we gotta make ah deal now, Mr. Bucks."

"Monte. Call me Monte." Monte Bucks presses play on the cell phone. He watched as the two jack boys got out of their car and started unloading. Then one of the jackers opened Sexy Duvall's driver side door. Pop! Pop!

***

"Bitch, you crazy...Ah...Ah...That might be some money...Ah, hello? Yo! Fo' real? Bet...Bet." The producers from *Love & Trap Muzik, Pittsburgh*, called Blocks N Bricks to let him know that they would be filming starting that Monday. "Yes! Mo' money in the bank, baby!"

"Who was that?"

"The producers from *Love & Trap Muzik*, we start filmin' Monday." Block N Bricks told the T.H.O.T.

"For real. Ah, that's what's up."

"Yup. I'ma hav'tah go get me ah new whip. Cause this season I'ma shine on 'em." Blocks N Bricks said.

"You gon' put me on the show?" The T.H.O.T asked.

"I might," Blocks N Bricks told her.

"Stop playin!"

"Probably not."

"Whatever! Come on, let's finish."

"Bitch! Didn't I just say I got business to handle. See that's why ya ass ain't gon' be on the show, cause you about a buck, and ah nigga like me is about ah buck!"

Blocks N Bricks knew that he was up against some stiff competition. The last season ended as other urban reality shows do, with arguments and fights displayed for the world to see on the reunion show. Unlike the other artist on the show, he had big shoes to fill. His father was a rap legend and expected him to always be on top of his game. In order to run the baton and win the first place medallion, Blocks N Bricks knew that he would have to find a balance between underground battle rap and mainstream success like his father did.

WHAT THE DEAL IS

When America pulled up to Pittsburgh's premiere *Mt. Washington* restaurant that overlooked the city, she saw the *Love & Trap Muzik's* security team and camera crew, and readied herself for filming. "Let's get it fo' moms," she told herself, fidgeting while checking her face in her visor mirror.

After being prompted, a slight touch of makeup, and being mic'd up, she entered the restaurant where *Love & Trap Muzik's* creator, Monte Bucks, sat. He was patiently waiting.

ACT ONE

SCENE A

For this particular shot, the producers brought out a section of the dining salon, and placed actors at surrounding tables in place of real patrons to make the background look authentic and natural.

INT. RESTAURANT-NIGHT

(America, Monte Bucks)

America steps into the restaurant. As America took her seat, an African American, full-figured waitress approached the dining table on cue, and placed water and menu's down on the table.

"I'll give you guys a few minutes to decide." The waitress states before turning to walk away.

Before the shooting began, America was told that she could order but they were only going to be there for the duration of the shoot. So after ordering, the colloquy between America and Monte Bucks evoked.

"First of all, thank you for meeting me. America, I'm sorry about what happened to ya grandmother and mother. What ah tragedy. And um, like I said on the phone, I'll be taking care of all funeral expenses, so don't worry about that.

"Thank you so much, Mr. Bucks. Thank you so much." America graciously replied.

I Need A Bawss In My Life

"No. Call me Monte, and you don't need to thank me. But...Umm, fuck it! I'ma just say it. I believe that a can put a great opportunity on the table for you."

"Mmm Okay. A great opportunity, huh?"

"Look, here's the deal, I would like for you to fill in for your mother this season. We'll have to add a separate contract for you, go through ah li'l paperwork, but like I said, I believe it's a great opportunity for your music to be heard. For us to speak out against violence. America..."

"I would love to be a part of the show."

"Would you?"

"Yes! I would love to. We start shooting in June, right?"

"That's what I wanted to talk to you about. We were supposed to start shooting in June, but due to your family's current affairs, the producers and I, wanted to start shooting in a couple of days. With your mother being shot and the funeral, we believe that this would be just what we need to boost our ratings. This would bring like ah 48

27

hours twist to ah Hip Hop reality show. Something that has never been done before. We could keep up with the investigation, and we're currently trying to work out a deal with the police force to get the interrogation tapes and the surveillance footage before TMZ gets it. So, what do you say?"

America's eyes wondered absently around the restaurant. Monte, waited patiently for an answer.

"We have to move fast." Monte stated hoping to get a quick answer.

"You talk about ratings, Mr. Bucks, but this is ah very serious matter to me and my family. And if I do this I know I'll receive a lot of backlash from social media, and my mom..." America replied.

"That's what we want, we want social media involved. And as far as your family, with the amount of money I'm gonna pay you."

"Ah, I'm pretty sure they'll understand. Look, this is an opportunity of ah lifetime, for you and me. You say

you wanna be ah star, well this is the kind of move that could make you ah star."

"True. And you say that the payoff is going to be…"

"Six figures. You'll be the highest paid cast member on the show. Plus, everything will revolve around you and your family." Monte Bucks, strokes his goatee, waiting for America to respond.

"Six figures?" America repeated Monte Bucks offer, nudging her shoulders. "Six figures could be ah hunid thousand."

"Or nine-hundred thousand."

"Make it seven-figures, and I'll throw in the footage," America proposed.

"Footage?!" Monte Bucks looks puzzled, stretches his neck, and bends his ear towards America as if he were trying to hear her clearer.

"Yea, I got the footage. There's three copies, I got two of 'em, and the police got the third. I gotta full version,

and ah shorter version that was recorded on ah cell phone. So what you wanna do, cause TMZ is offering six figures?"

"Bullshit!" Monte bucks sits back in his seat and folds his arms across his chest.

"Mr. Bucks..."

"Monte, call me Monte."

"Okay. Well Monte, I wouldn't bullshit ya. Now being that you're willing to up the date of recording the show, I know that you know that time is of the essence. So using ya words, we gotta move fast." America used Monte's words on him to get her point across.

"Ha, ha, ha." Monte Bucks laughs, impressed with America's business savvy.

"So do we have ah deal?" America asked Monte Bucks, pulling out her cell phone, and sitting it on the table.

"Daaammn!" Monte Bucks exclaims loudly, not believing what he was seeing.

The Jacker was blown backwards. Then the footage stops.

"So do we have ah deal, seven figures?"

"You're ah good business woman. The world is gonna love you, America Duvall," Monte Bucks said, taking a sip of the water sitting in front of him. "We gotta deal. I'll have my people write everything up. You'll have ah million in ah hour, but I'ma need that other footage."

"No problem, it's yours." America pushes her chair back from the table.

"Hey though, one question...How did you get the footage? Did Dominican give it to you?"

"Nah, my people got it fo' me."

BANKROLL FRESH

All we do is trap...All we do is trap...All we do is trap... All we do is trap

I wouldn't be where I was if I ain't fuckin' trap

I don't leave the trap

I stay down just to make it happen.

Stay down to get it/ Grinded from ah fifty/Then I got up/

I had my niggas wit' me...

"Thump...Thump...Thump...Thump," Listening to Bankroll Fresh, Smack Down took a hammer to a kilogram of cocaine. Then took a razor and cut an X into the duct tape the kilo was wrapped in. Removing several large blocks of cocaine from the kilo, he placed them on a scale, and weighed them up until the scale read, one hundred twenty-six grams.

After placing the 4-1-2 into two thick Ziploc bags, Smack Down placed it on newspaper before pounding the work with the hammer some more, and used the bottom of his brown transparent *Vison Ware* pot to crush it.

Smack Down grinded the chunks of consolidated cocaine into a powder, prepping it to be cooked up. Leaving the hammer, cocaine, and pot on the floor, he ripped open a yellow box of *Baking Soda* and poured what he believed to be four and a half ounces into a Ziploc bag. It was forty-nine grams off so he added more soda until the scale read, one hundred thirty-three grams. He added an extra seven grams because he knew that at least seven grams would burn off in the cook.

Placing his pot on the stove, he ignited the fire under the pot, and put it on medium. Waiting as the powder heated up, he slowly stirred it, and crushed up the remaining chunks of compressed yayo. He added the soda, and stirred the powders together. Then he used a squirt gun, and squirted a small amount of water on the product. Its aroma lit up the room. After the work started to bubble, he used a butter knife to stir it up. The kitchen smelled of burning glue.

Working his wrist in a 360-degree motion, he watched as the oil and soda turned into a thick white paste. After turning off the fire, he plugged up the kitchen sink, took a bag of ice out of the freezer, dumped it into the sink, and ran a stream of cold water into the sink. Then he placed the pot of coca into the sink, and watched as it hardened.

Using his hand, he scooped ice water into the pot. Once he was sure that the coca was hard, he used a toothbrush, and scrubbed the soda residue off of the top of the coca, and then turned the water off.

Taking a knife, he carefully stabbed into the pot of product, causing it to crack in several directions. Then he used the knife, and maneuvered it around the border of the pot, separating the coca from the pot in large, chunky parts. Placing the large, chunky pieces into a Ziploc bag, he weighed it, and watched as the numbers on the scale shot up to two hundred fifty-four grams. He had turned four and a half ounces into a quarter of a kilogram.

As Smack Down was busy doing his thing, his phone rang.

'Yo, who this? Oh, okay. What's up, doe? Ah, that...That's what's up. Yea, okay. I'm looking forward to it...Cool." Smack Down had received his call back from *Love & Trap Muzik*. They told him filming would start that Monday.

Leaning back on to the kitchen counter, he looked over at the coca he had just cooked up. "I gotta make this music shit work," he told himself.

Walking into the living room where his crew smoked Sour Diesel and popped pills, listening to Future, he demanded their attention. "YO! YO! Turn that shit down." After the music was turned to a low level, he made his announcement. "We start filming the show Monday, they just called. This season, let's turn the fuck up!"

***

"Two platinum albums and ah nigga's still strugglin' out this bitch. Three mill', four mill' ain't shit out this bitch! You got rap niggas out here sittin' on two, three-hunid million. Ma'fuckas don't know shit look good on the outside these mansions, these cars, these bitches, the jewelry, but on the inside eh'thang reckless. That nigga Bigg ain't die with ah hunid million, that nigga Pac ain't die wit' no hunid million. Them niggas is still the best in the game. Me, I ain't try'na be the best in the game. Me, I need to die wit' at least ah hunid million. I need to be up when I go, nigga got kids. I'm talking legacy shit." Mr. Frosty Blow spoke to his employees at a boardroom meeting. They watched him as he paced back and forth, taking in his every word. "This season... This season, though, we gots to dominate! We gotta make moves, major moves. Moves like this gon' be our last season on the show. We got mad talent on the show, niggas like DQ Dawg doin' his thang, Blocks N Bricks, Smack Down and his boys doin' they thang, but we gotta out do 'em all!" Mr. Frosty Blow encouraged his team. He had gotten his call back from the *Love & Trap Muzik, Pittsburgh*, producers, and he wanted to make sure they were all on point, and understood the importance of winning. "So what we got lined up, what we got planned this season?" He asked, taking his seat at the head of the boardroom table.

Armoni, his top assistant, looked through her notes, and stood up. "We got you a listen session late Monday night with Boom Bap, and another one Tuesday with Making Hitz, both sessions will be filmed by the show."

"Okay," Mr. Frosty Blow nodded his head up and down, waiting for more.

"Yea, I know you're looking for that new sound, and at the same time you want the promo from the show so I wanted you to be the first on the show to meet with them. They're both hot right now."

"That's what's up. Cars?"

"I got you ah Lambo truck. I was goin' to get you the Bent truck, but after I made calls to all the cast members asking them what they would be driving, I found out Blocks N Bricks will be driving that this season, and I know you don't wanna be driving the same thing as him."

"Hell no! Good shit. Shows?"

Armoni flipped through her notes. "We gotta twenty-five city tour coming up. I didn't want to book you for a whole lot of tour dates because of the show. Ah, and we gotta do ah show here. Dominican Flames called she wants you to perform at her club. She wants to do something with the show. You know, after the shooting she got a lot of bad press. So she wanna show that the spot is still poppin', and that's probably why the show is premiering the teaser there."

"They are?"

"Yea. I thought I told you."

"No."

"Oh, I'm sorry. I thought I did."

"Nah, but look, let me ask you this. Will the show be filming us when we go on our tour dates?"

"If we want to record ah show outside of the city, we'll have to pay traveling expenses for the camera crew."

"What?"

"Ha ha, yea. Monte Bucks told me that himself. But anything within the city that we do is covered."

"Alright, cool. Did you get the flowers for Sexy and America?"

"Yup, I took care of that. By the way, America is headlining the season."

"WHAT?! What you mean headlining the season? How'd that happen?"

"I-don't-know. I tried to get some info on it, but everybody's being hush-hush about it. We actually start recording Monday at her people's gravesite, and it's mandatory for everybody to be there. At least for the recording of the show."

"Mandatory?"

"Mandatory! From what I gathered before the actual funeral they want all of y'all to go to the gravesite. They're goin' to hire paid fill-in actors to make it look official. Then if you want you'll attend the funeral, where they'll continue recording. But they're not going back to the gravesite, they don't want to offend the Duvall family, and that's why they're doin' their own shoot beforehand.

"These fake ass ma'fuckas. They all about the ratings, ain't they."

"I mean that's what pays the bills."

"Yea, you right."

"Okay, so tomorrow everybody is scheduled to meet with Monte Bucks, and the producers of the show. They're going to brief everybody. Um, they asked us to tell all of your followers to go to their web page Tuesday night. They're going to promo the new season then. We'll see it at the Teaser Premiere Party they're having it at Dominican's club, Tuesday."

"Damn, they ain't playin'. They try'na get the ball rollin'."

"Yes. They're ready to go."

"Hell yea. What else?"

Armoni looked through her notes. "That's about it right now."

"Call a stylist, I wanna make sure my shit's right at the premiere."

"Already on that. After the meeting with Monte Bucks, you'll meet with the stylist."

"So why ain't you add that?"

"I-I..."

"Ya ass is slippin', Money. Don't make me get rid of ya ass...Ha ha ha."

"Yea right!"

Money was a nickname, Mr. Frosty gave his number one girl. He would never get rid of her, she played a major part in his success. Without her his whole world would fall apart.

THE V.I.P.s

Monte Bucks sat inside of his Maybach, listening to Maybach Music III, waiting for his celebrity guest to land on the tarmac. He had flown several artists to Pittsburgh to attend his Teaser Party, which was being held at Dominican Flame's nightclub, *Reflections*. They had arrived hours earlier and was handled by his assistants. But for these particular mega stars he sent his personal Learjet, his Dassault Falcon 7X to make sure they traveled in the luxurious standard they were accustomed to. It was the same kind of Learjet Bill Gates owned. "If it's good enough for Bill, it's good enough for Bucks," he would tell people.

Sipping on his D'Usse, and smoking his Cohiba cigar, he looked through a list of cast members that were selected to be on the show on his iPad. The email that was sent to him showed a picture of the cast members and gave a descriptive account of who they were.

America Duvall (Daughter of Sexy Duvall), hit the studio on a guess appearance of Love & Trap Muzik,

Pittsburgh, and set the booth ablaze. After her mother, Sexy Duval, was shot five times, not only did America beef up her street goons, she stocked up on her rhyme arsenal. Her plans are to take over the ghetto-fabulous Rap Reality Show that shot her mother to strip-club and national stardom. But don't get it lucked up, America didn't come to hitch a ride off of her mother's star, she came to take claim of her own meteoric rise, and reign as Hip Hop's new Queen.

Mr. Frosty Blow: The hustler turned Trap Music god, claims to own the streets of Pittsburgh. With two platinum albums to date, he battles with rap rivals like Smack Down and street thugs alike to keep his crown, as he dodges the Feds, and their Federal Indictments.

Boom Bap: The Pittsburgh Native, is a legendary female producer that spends most of her time crafting timeless hits, and in between producing and business meetings, the melodic mastermind is behind the scene of some of the most adorn records; sets aside time to mentor Rap Idols and Crooners alike. All while continuing to captivate the ears of Urban and Pop audiences, decade after decade.

Dominican, Flames: Hailing all the way from Brooklyn New York, Dominican Flames' parents made their way to Pittsburgh in the late eighties, where they faced Federal Indictments for Drug Distribution and Racketeering, from which they both received lengthy sentences. But now the daughter of the Drug Lord Dynasty, owns one of the biggest strip clubs in Pennsylvania, and manages strippers and up and coming rap artist like Sexy Duvall and her daughter, America.

DQ Dawg: A trap veteran turned author that has made millions in the music industry is now taking over the publishing world, one book at a time. reinventing himself after a seven-year hiatus, the rapper once known as Rah Zigga, has once again shot to the top of the charts with his new single, "She Like It From The Baaack!" Torn between his record contract and publishing deal he manages to stay on top of both with a number one single and number one urban novel, he balances both careers like a checkbook filled with zeros.

Blocks N Bricks: Mr. live through it all, is taking on all comers, new and old. The son of one of Hip Hop's most revered lyricist, Dre Dog Ski, carries the torch scorching anybody that gets in his way. Blazing his way up the charts in pursuit of the longevity and accolades that made his father a commercial and mainstream success.

Making Hitz: Is a high caliber producer with ties to the music industry's most majestic couple, King and Queen Carter. As the head of his own record label he helps artists get recognized and released. Solidifying their penmanship on the lines of huge record deals. The rapper, song writer, producer is a triple threat. Starting as a pupil of Boom Bap's musical elite, the prodigy Making Hitz took production advice and ran with it. With close to 200 chart topping smashes to date in three short years, he has arrived and plans to conquer.

Smack Down: With just a month left before his independent album release, the Smack Dizzy Boys' boss has blessed his fans with a hundred freestyle videos, racking up twenty million views on YouTube. As a battle rapper he goes at some of the top artists in the industry and steps on underground rappers in the streets. With braggadocio sixteens he crushes and kills all competition on the way to the top. In doing so, Smack Down has attracted record labels and executives to himself like vultures to a dead carcass. Caught up in a multi-million dollar bidding war the gritty underground king has to decide between staying in the street and the industry.

Leaning back, Monte Bucks looked up at the twinkly celestial ceiling of his Maybach, feeling good about what his cast of artists had to offer the world. Then he was alerted by a message that contained a *TMZ* link. "FUCK!" Monte Bucks was upset by what he saw on his iPad, *TMZ* had gotten their hands on the surveillance footage.

***

The funeral was over, the dead had been buried, the blood that stained *Reflections'* parking lot had been washed away and business went on as usual. Dominican Flames put together a Red Carpet Event to celebrate the first day of shooting *Love& Trap Muzik, Pittsburgh*, and she was premiering in the teaser that the producers of the show wanted them all to promote on their social media pages.

The *Love & Trap Muzik, Pittsburgh* party was the number one destination to celebrate the fall's upcoming season. More than one thousand guest attended, including the cast of *Love & Hip Hop New York, Atlanta and LA, Housewives of Atlanta, and Empire.*

The invigorating night spotlighted presenting Jay Z's streaming company *Tidal.* Jay Z himself was not scheduled to be there. It was said Jay Z told Monte Bucks, "Reality shows ain't my thing,". Instead he had sent a few of his representatives in place of himself. But Jay Z's absence did not dim the limelight. Plenty of other mega stars like Kanye West and Kim K., Jeezy, Nicki Minaj, Rick Ross and Drake lit up the night's event. The night was star studded, and the Cast of *Love & Trap Muzik, Pittsburgh*, refused to be outshined.

Outside of the club, exotic cars were being valeted. A crowd of fans screamed and yelled whenever their favorite celebrity pulled up to the Red Carpet and exited their steel chariots.

Flashbulbs lit up and popped, camera lenses shuttered as they flickered, lighting up the crowd that surrounded the club's entrance like strobe lights. A man with what seemed to be homosexual stood on the inside of the entrance with a clipboard in his hand, checking off the invited guest, V.I.P.s and stars of hit reality TV shows. The Red Carpet runway led them inside of Reflections.

After making it through the flashing lights and sea of screaming fans requesting selfies and autographs, they were greeted by more paparazzi hoopla. Inside they posed for a sequence of pictures in front of a multi-name branded backdrop that displayed the names of sponsors surrounding the *Love& Trap Muzik, Pittsburgh* moniker that was printed on its canvas. Hip Hop magazines, entertainment news, and bloggers were there to capture every moment.

Around 7:00 P.M. is when the cast members started pulling up. Blocks N Bricks pulled up in a powder blue, cocaine white, gutted Bentley truck; Mr. Frosty Blow pulled behind him in a red Lambo Truck; Boom Bap, the legendary female producer, pulled up behind them in a black and yellow Ferrari Laferrari, sitting on matching colored shoes; Making Hitz pulled up behind her in his BMW 18. Smack Down and the Smack Dizzy Boys, crept up in back of them in a royal blue, silver striped Series II dropped Phantom. It was like a battle of the ballers affair. Everybody bought their "A" game.

Paparazzi, including *TMZ*, simultaneously snapped photos, and asked questions as their cameras captured the moment. Then America pulled up in some shit no one had ever seen before. It was a root beer colored low-slung beast, that was all power and speed, a *Ronn Motor Company* dropped Scorpion, that Ronn Maxwell had flown to her from California for the show. As she stepped from behind the Lamborghini doors that opened like a set of wings, all eyes and cameras lit up, and was all over her.

"America...America...America." The crowd yelled.

America waved at them and took pictures with some of the fans. She accepted their condolences, but she ignored questions about her mother as she made her way into the club.

"Where da fuck dat bitch get da money fo' dat shit?" Smack Down asked his man Hitter B.

"I don't know. But she keep poppin' like dat, anotha bitch gon' get jacked," Hitter B. said, hating on America.

"Ha ha ha...Nigga you crazy." Smack Down laughed at his man not really taking him serious.

After taking pictures for the media, America was mic'd up and escorted to the V.I.P section. "Mr. Bucks wants you to share his booth," the hostess told her. Two barmaids with sparkling bottles of Ace of Spades followed them to the upper level of the club. The area was kept clear. The huge, muscular man guarding the booth nodded his head at America and unsnapped the velvet rope that blocked the entrance.

"Bring me twenty stacks of ones," America told the hostess.

"Yeezy Yeezy Yeezy, just jumped over Jumpman

Yeezy Yeezy Yeezy, just jumped over Jumpman

Yeezy Yeezy Yeezy, I feel so accomplished

I den talked a lot of shit, but I just did the numbers..."

America bobbed her head as Kanye's song *Facts* started playing. Grabbing up a bottle of Ace she started snaking her head side to side, jerking her body to the beat as she raised her baller bottle.

"...If Nike didn't have Drizzy, man, they wouldn't have nothin'"

America looked over at the V.I.P area that Drake and the 0-V-0 crew was in, she smiled, watching Drake recite Kanye's lyrics, as most of the club did. Kanye's *Life of Pablo* CD was the hottest CD on the street.

"...Yeezy Yeezy Yeezy, they line up for days

I ain't drop an album, but the shoes went platinum..."

Then America's eyes widened. Totally in shock, she cocked her head back, awestricken. She was fucked up to see Kanye in the DJ booth performing the song live. She went crazy, raising her baller bottle to him. The *Love & Trap Muzik, Pittsburgh* camera crew captured it all.

"...2020 lima run the whole election..." America rapped Kanye's lyrics along with him. Popping a Xanny, she chased it with the Ace, feeling herself. It was a big night.

Towards the end of Kanye's song, Drake made his way to the DJ booth, his crew parted the sea of party goers for him. The *Love& Trap Muzik* camera crew followed Drake through the crowd, while others filmed Kanye, America, and other cast members while all of this was happening. All together there were twelve camera men recording for the show.

"...Nike Nike treat employees just like slaves

gave Lebron a Mill' not to run away..."

Kanye continued to rap, wrapping his arm around Drake's neck, greeting him. Drake rapped every lyric with him. Then it was Drake's turn. After *Facts*, the DJ Schizo played Drake and Future's Jumpman. Kanye passed the mic to Drake, and started zoning out, doing his dance.

"Jumpman Jumpman Jumpman, dem boys up to sometin

they just spent two or three weeks out the country..."

As Drake rapped, America noticed a big commotion in the crowd. She stopped dancing when she saw what all the commotion was about, and who was approaching the

V.I.P section she was in. It was Dominican Flames and Making Hitz escorting Jay Z and Beyoncé, Monte Bucks trailed behind them.

America wondered why she was the only one allowed in the booth, now she knew why. "Aaaah, oh my God!" She jumped up and down when she saw the power couple. Jay Z and Beyoncé smiled at her.

"Look at this bitch," Dominican Flames said to herself. "Nothing like her mom. If the bitch wants me to manage her she gon' hav'tah chill wit' this groupie acting shit." She continued to judge America. Truth was all of the cast members of *Love & Trap Muzik, Pittsburgh*, was mad that America came out of nowhere and took the lead role on the show.

America had been around celebrities before, her mother had introduced her to a lot of them, but none of this magnitude. There were a lot of stars in the building that night, but Jay Z and Beyoncé were on another level. Seeing them she was unable to hold her composure. She, like everyone else, was told that Jay Z wasn't coming. So to see him and his wife Beyoncé was mind blowing.

Monte Bucks had unsuccessfully tried to convince Jay Z to come, but couldn't. But after talking to Dominican Flames about his dilemma she spoke to her father, and all of a sudden Jay Z was on board. Come to find, Dominican Flames' father, Brooklyn Pete, and Jay Z were close friends. So after speaking with Brooklyn Pete, Jay Z called Dominican Flames, personally, and assured her that he would be there. Dominican Flames wasn't that impressed. To her, her father was the real star. He was the one Jay Z spoke highly off, and he was the one that got Jay Z to attend the Teaser Party. And not only did Jay Z show up, he brought his wife with him.

Jay Z and Beyoncé were used to America's reaction to them. As Jay Z maneuvered his way around the V.I.P section, Beyoncé held her arms out to give America a welcoming hug. "Sorry to hear about your family," Beyoncé said to America, embracing her tightly.

"Thank you, Bee." America replied, breaking their hug, still clasped at the hands.

"Come on let's have some fun in this bitch!" Beyoncé said.

"Ha ha ha, ya real as'shit, Bee." America didn't expect Queen Bey to be so down to earth.

As Dominican Flames and Monte Bucks discussed what time to show the Teaser, Jay Z and Beyoncé, greeted the other stars that came to the booth to pay homage to the billion-dollar couple.

Other cast members watched as Rick Ross wrapped his arm around Jay's neck, and Jeezy joked with him causing him to grin that million dollar smile that Jay Z's true friends were familiar with.

"I can't stand that muthafucka. Ewww, I hate him," Boom Bap said to her girl, gritting on Making Hitz as he mingled with Kanye West.

She knew that they were talking about getting together. She had taught Making Hitz mostly everything he knew. She had even occasionally opened her legs to him. And a knife in her back was the only thanks she got. Lighting her blunt filled with Khalifa Kush, she put it to her mouth, took a strong pull, and exhaled never taking her eyes off of the one that got away.

For America the night couldn't get any better, she wished her mother could have been there. She took selfies with Drake, Nicki Minaj, Jay Z and Beyoncé, and posted them on her Facebook and Instagram pages. "A Star Amongst Stars," she Tweeted.

"Let's get down to the DJ booth," Monte Bucks told Dominican Flames. "We goin' down to the DJ Booth," he told America. "We about to show the Teaser...You ready?"

"Yes. Hey, thank you." America thanked Monte Bucks.

"No problem. I told you this was a big opportunity for you...Hey, did you see the footage on *TMZ*?" Monte Bucks asked.

"No... I didn't give it to 'em."

"Oh, I know you didn't. Someone from the police department did. But we still good...Let me get down here," Monte Bucks said, making his way to the DJ booth.

"Man, look at that dick eatin' bitch. She all kissin' dat nigga's ass." Hitter B said to Smack Down, nudging his head towards America and Monte Bucks talking.

"Yea, some'in's goin' on. She gets fifteen minutes of air time last season, now she's the center of attention. All in da V.I.P wit' Jay Z, an' dem other ma'fuckas, an' shit," Smack Down said, shaking his head.

"Fifteen Minutes of Fame, now she thinks she da shit, an' shit! She gon' have me put ah end to dat shit. And I ain't goin' out like dat nigga that hit her mother up. Fo' real. I'ma get all dat paper." Hitter B. said.

"Dis fool trippin'," Smack Down thought. He felt some way about America taking the lead role on the show, but it only made him want to step his game up. Besides that, he liked America, and was cool with her mother. He respected their hustle.

INT. REFLECTIONS NIGHTCLUB NIGHT

Monte Bucks and Dominican Flams entered the DJ booth. DJ Schizo makes an announcement to get the clubs attention, then gives the microphone to Monte Bucks; who introduces the *Love & Trap Muzik, Pittsburgh*, Teaser.

"Everybody...Everybody, let me get your attention. We about to sho the Teaser. Everybody listen up," DJ Schizo yelled into the mic.

Monte Bucks clears his throat. "Um um, I wanna thank everyone for coming out tonight, Jay Z, Beyoncé, Kanye and Kim, Drake and 0-V-0, Nicki Minaj, Jeezy, Rick Ross, and all of the cast members from all of the other reality shows in the building. Most of all I would like to thank the sponsors, Jay Z and the team at Tidal. And Dominican Flames for putting this together, give it up to Dominican Flames."

The crowd cheered as Monte Bucks made his announcement.

"This year we're going to show our asses, display a lot of talent, and address some social issues. At the same time turn up! Dominican Flames..."

"Roll that shit!" Dominican Flames shouted as the crowd cheered.

Huge monitors began to show the Teaser for the upcoming season of *Love & Trap Muzik, Pittsburgh.*

Sexy Duvall is rushed down a hospital hallway on a gurney. Doctors try desperately to revive her.

SOUND: HEARTBEAT

Sexy Duvall (dying voice) Some kill for Power...

EXT. REFLECTIONS PARKING LOT-Continuous

Two jack boys jump out of their car and approached Sexy Duvall's car with their weapons drawn. One jack boy starts shooting.

FX: GUNSHOTS

FADE OUT/FADE IN

SOUND: HEARTBEAT

Sexy Duvall (Dying voice) ...Some run Empires

Some battle for dominance...

Two golden microphones face each other in the spotlight center stage.

Sexy Duvall (dying voice) ...Through acts of betrayal infamy is born...

EXT. HOSPITAL ROOM 718

FADE OUT/FADE IN

SOUND: HEARTBEAT

The door to the hospital Room 718 slowly opens.

Sexy Duvall (Dying voice) ...Ones last breath leads to another's new beginning...

FADE OUT/FADE IN

SOUND: HEARTBEAT EXT. CHURCH

The cast of Love & Trap Muzik, Pittsburgh, leave a church, following behind a casket being carried by six pallbearers to a line of black hearses.

Sexy Duvall (Dying voice) ...Some rise from the trap to become the most powerful in the industry...

FADE OUT/FADE IN

SOUND: HEARTBEAT EXT. GRAVESIDE

The cast of Love & Trap Muzik, Pittsburgh, stand at a graveside. America steps forward, and drops a black rose unto a casket as it's lowered into the ground.

FADE OUT/FADE IN

SOUND: HEARTBEAT

EXT. STAGE

The cast of Love & Trap Muzik, Pittsburgh, walk towards two golden microphones facing each other in the spotlight center stage.

Sexy Duvall (Dying voice) ...Us, we run shit for the love of trap music and our City...

FADE OUT/FADE IN

SOUND: HEARTBEAT EXT. STAGE

The cast of Love & Trap Muzik, Pittsburgh, continue to walk towards two golden microphones facing each other in the spotlight center stage. America and Mr. Frosty grab their microphones. The entire cast turns towards the cameras.

FADE OUT/FADE. IN

SOUND: HEARTBEAT

INT. HOSPITAL ROOM 718

The camera slowly creeps inside of hospital room 718, until it comes to someone in a hospital bed. The camera slowly pans upward over the body of the person lying in the hospital bed. Finally, Sexy Duvall is revealed with her eyes closed.

FADE OUT

SOUND: HEARTBEAT-Continuous FADE IN

INT. HOSPITAL BED

(Sexy Duvall)

Sexy Duvall (Dying voice/eyes open) ...Welcome to Pittsburgh.

FADE OUT

LOVE & TRAP MUZIK, PITTSBURGH

The audience in the club erupted. Monte Bucks and Dominican Flames hugged.

"Who gave you the footage?" She asked. Monte Bucks didn't reveal his source but his eyes led to America.

Looking into the crowd as they applauded, America and Dominican Flames locked eyes. America raised her bottle to Dominican Flames. Dominican Flames rolled her eyes, turned her head and looked at a smiling Monte Bucks. Monte Bucks didn't look at the situation the way Dominican Flames did. He looked at it as a great opportunity to boost ratings, she looked at it as an act of betrayal.

Putting on a fake smile Dominican Flames started lapping along with the crowd. It wasn't the time to act a fool. Monte Bucks had made it clear that the night was to be drama free, and anyone that caused drama would be immediately cut from the show. So she took everything in without lashing out, but she definitely planned on getting revenge. Betrayal was something that she didn't tolerate.

COPS & BALLERS

Smack Down sat up in his bed and paused for the time being. The vibrations and alerts from his cell phone woke him from his trance. He was thinking about making two, no more than three more moves before getting out of the game. It had been three days since he had spoken to his connect. The night before anxiety had got the best of him, and he sent his connect a text message before he fell asleep. But there was no response. Knowing his connect was still in motion if that ever happened, he didn't bother to call or text again. If anything ever went wrong his connect's lawyer would contact him, and that wasn't the case so he wasn't worried, he was just being impatient.

Checking his phone, Smack Down smiled. His connect had sent him a message, "7:00 P.M.," was all the message said. The meeting spot was predestined, and the money had already been exchanged. All Smack Down had to do was pick up his work. Normally, it was just as easy as that, but lately Smack Down had the Love & Trap Muzik,

Pittsburgh's, camera crew following him. He would have to get rid of them before he went to pick his work up.

After erasing his connect's message, he sat his cell phone on the hotel's lampstand, and looked over at the two strippers he had brought to the hotel with him, Cinnamon and Sugar. Cinnamon was Cuban and Lebanese, 34C-26-36, she was from Brick City, New Jersey, and Sugar was Italian and Irish, 34B-27-46, and she was from New York. They both worked at Reflections and danced as a team.

Grabbing Cinnamon's ass, Smack Down shook her.

"Hm?" She groaned.

Smack Down shook her again, and she groaned again, "Hm?" This time, she turned and looked at him with one eye open, her head resting on her folded arms. She was just as horny as Smack Down, but she was still half-sleep. And all of them were aware of the Love & Trap Muzik, Pittsburgh, cameraman recording them. The show had contacted Smack Down an hour before going to the hotel to set up. Smack Down had paid the girls to make sure they gave the cameraman a show that he would eventually have to edit.

Smack Down felt Cinnamon's hand climb up his leg and take a hold of his manhood underneath the covers. "Yo know what time it is." Smack Down blurted out. Thinking of Cinnamon's nipple and clit piercing helped him keep his dick hard. As Cinnamon stroked him, his ass clinched a few times, and his man piece grew more and more as if each clinch added an inch to his cock.

Reaching over, Smack Down cupped and squeezed her expensive tit. "Oh, ewww," Cinnamon moaned. She held his dick erect and swiped her tongue back and forth over his dick head before entering him inside of her mouth. The warmth and wetness of her mouth caused Smack Down's eyes roll to the back of his head. Cinnamon's head jerked up and down his dick. She liked the way his pre-cum tasted and loved swallowing his sweet, savory cum.

Awakened by the sounds of morning sex, Sugar joined in by kissing Cinnamon from her neck down, leaving a wet trail of kisses down her back to her ass. Cinnamon looked back and tooted her ass up to be eaten. Sugar didn't disappoint, she spread her ass cheeks and stuck her tongue in Cinnamon's asshole as far as she could.

Cinnamon parted her lips and spit saliva on Smack Down's dick like syrup on a breakfast sausage, then she ate all she could eat.

The cameraman's hand found its way down his joggers. He began to masturbate as he recorded the best scene he had ever recorded for the reality show. "This is the best scene ev-urrr." He said in a fiendish whisper.

"Yes...Yes, eat that ass, bitch!" Cinnamon looked back and told Sugar as she tongue-fucked her asshole, and her fingers slipped in and out of her slippery cunt.

"Oh baby...oh baby...eat me...EAT ME!" Cinnamon managed to get out with a mouth full of thick, pulsating meat pumping in and out of her throat.

Grabbing Cinnamon by a fist full of her weave at the back of her head, Smack Down pulled her from his dick and met her mouth with a passionate French kiss. He released her hair, and her dick sucker went back the work on his dick. Smack Down crawled back from her trying to escape submission, but her mouth sought after his cum shooter like a fugitive on the run.

"Mmmm, muthafucka. You gon' cum in this mouth," Cinnamon said in Spanish.

"Oooh...mmm...shit!" Hearing her say that made the cameraman bust all over himself. Hearing the cameraman cumming, Sugar went over to him and pulled down his cum-stained joggers and boxers and began to suck cum from his dick. She licked the white glaze that ran down between his legs and balls, "Fuucck! Uh-uh-uh...Ugh!"

"Ha ha ha," Sugar laughed at the cameraman as he fell backwards and dropped his camera.

Ignoring what was going on behind them, Cinnamon and Smack Down worked together. Her mouth sucked, spit, and slurped while he fucked her mouth, pumping his hips, harder and harder.

Gaining his composure, the cameraman picked up his camera and continued filming. Sugar sat in a chair and finger-fucked herself. She watched Cinnamon suck Smack Down's dick until she came. "Fffff-uuck, yes...Yes...Mm...Mm."

The intensity of what was going on made the cameraman's heart beat faster and faster. He could feel his dick getting hard again. The sight of Sugar cumming and Smack Down pounding Cinnamon's mouth turned him on.

Sugar slowly walked over to the bed and started humping on Cinnamon's fat ass in the doggy style position. It looked as if she was packing a dick. Cinnamon threw her ass back at her and moaned as if she were getting fucked by Sugar.

"Cum daddy...Cum in that bitches' mouth...Cum in that nasty bitches' mouth...Cum in that slut's mouth!" Sugar told Smack Down, looking him in the eyes, and grinding pussies with Cinnamon.

"Eewww...Yooooo! Here...Here...Ah...Here it comes," Smack Down struggled to get out.

"Yea daddy, cum in her mouth." Sugar said making her way to his dick, wanting to taste him just as much as Cinnamon did.

"You slut...You SLUT! Ew you...You." Smack Down released a thick, hot wad of cum into Cinnamon's mouth. She caught it all in her mouth and the back of her throat. Once Smack Down's dick stopped cumming, Cinnamon came up from his dick, and kissed Sugar, sharing her creamy treat.

"Ew, y'all some nasty ass bitches, and I love it," Smack Down said, wiping his face with his hand.

***

Inside of his office, at the head of the squad room, Bureau Commander, Lieutenant Percy Combs, had been browsing the internet for thirty minutes. His fingers swiped through files and footage looking for clues that would lead him to the second suspect in Case #1220, the Sexy Duvall case. Sitting down his iPad, he took out a cigarette from a pack that sat on his desk, and lit it. Never taking his eyes off of Sexy Duvall's Facebook profile picture, he exhaled cigarette smoke into the air space of his office. Placing the cigarette in an ashtray, he finger-swiped through Sexy Duvall's page. Checking her post, he stopped at a digital copy of a flyer promoting the Love & Trap Muzik, Pittsburgh, Teaser Party. Clicking on the comments, he noticed most of them were get well messages, prayers, and condolence notes attached to prayer hand pictures, or blue skies and doves. Swiping downward, he came to a post of pictures from the party. The first picture was that of a female that looked similar to Sexy, posing with Jay Z and Beyoncé. At that time, he didn't know that the female posing with the rappers, as he thought them to be, was Sexy Duvall's daughter, America Duvall. Opening up another window on his iPad, he Googled Love& Trap Muzik, Pittsburgh, Teaser Party, and was sent to a YouTube link. Pressing play on the link, he sat back, and waited for the video to start.

"THIS IS SEXY DUVALL FROM LOVE & TRAP MUZIK, PITTSBURGH. WE JUST WATCHED THE TEASER, SHIT WAS CRAZY! MY MOM, SEXY DUVALL, DID THE VOICE OVER ON IT... I MEAN WE BOUT THIS LIFE, WE TURNT UP IN THIS BITCH. WE..." America said, yelling over the loud music playing in the background, before she was cut off by Smack Down.

"YEA, WE TURNT ALL THE WAY UP IN DIS MUTHAFUCKA! WE GOT JAY Z, RICK ROSS, YEEZY, DRAKE, MAAAN LOOK, SHOUT OUT TO MONTE BUCKS, THE SMACK DIZZY BOYZ..."

Lt. Combs, stopped the video, and swiped downward then clicked on another video titled, "Sexy Duvall Goes In". It was a video of Sexy Duvall dancing at a strip club. Watching the video got the lieutenant's dick hard. Picking up his cigarette, he took a pull and exhaled from his nose. Fighting with his erection, he tugged at his crouch. "I need some pussy bad," he said shaking his head.

KNOCK! KNOCK! KNOCK!

"You wanted to see us L-T?" Robbery-Homicide detective, Castaneda Gordy, asked knocking on the door of Lt. Combs' office, opening it without being asked. Behind her was her partner, Robbery-Homicide detective, Ray Burnam. They stood in the entrance of the office.

"Which one of y'all would like to explain this?" Lt. Combs asked lying his iPad down in front of the detectives to view. Standing up, he took another pull of his cigarette that was burning close to the butt and smashed it out in his ashtray, waiting for an answer. "I take it that you muthafuckas ain't surprised. Now explain this shit. How did TMZ get their hands on our evidence, how did our evidence get all over the internet?!" Lt. Combs asked in a

73

harsher voice, gazing angrily at the two investigators for what seemed to be an eternity. The expression on his face was a cross between disappointment and displeasure.

The leak of the footage confirmed to many the patterns governing the corrupt police department of Pittsburgh. Knowing that they were guilty of leaking the footage, neither of the detectives said a word at first, and was willing to go down together.

"You two have been bringing a lot of heat on me, lately. This is the last time..." Lt. Combs paused, looking both of them in the eyes. The last fuckin' time I'ma warn y'all asses. Because the next time y'all names come across my desk y'all gon' be pushing pens like ah muthafuckin bread maker. Y'all understand me?"

"L-T..." Taking in all the critical backlash she could take, detective Gordy tried to explain their position. The two detectives were even willing to give the lieutenant a percentage of the fifty-thousand they had made off of the footage, but Lt. Combs wouldn't allow her to get a full sentence out.

"But..."

"Oh, know you don't! You don't get to talk now. Because I know you gon' try tah run some of ya bullshit on me, Castaneda. I know how hard it is to fight the temptations out here to make ah couple extra dollars. I know the pay cuts, and the cut back on extra hours got y'all in ah tight spot. I've been doin' this shit for thirty years, so I know what's up. But I know y'all don't want Internal Affairs breathin' down y'all necks again. Making y'all's lives ah livin' hell for the third time, now do you?" Lt. Combs asked, getting close up on detective Ray Barnum, his breath smelled of coffee and cigarettes.

"L-T?" Detective Gordy said, tired of hearing the lieutenant run his mouth.

"WHAT, CASTANEDA?!"

"We've identified the suspect on the Sexy Duvall case." Detective Gordy was finally able to tell her superior officer.

The room got quiet. Lt. Combs took his seat, and leaned back.

"You've identified the second suspect? Ha ha, you guys have saved ya asses once again. Because y'all was definitely about to be suspended," Lt. Combs said accepting a manila envelope from detective Burnam. "So this is our guy, huh, Andrew Kaus?" He questioned feeling relieved. The pressure from the Stop the Violence Groups in Pittsburgh was causing tension.

Not only did Sexy Duvall get shot five times, but her mother had died from a massive heart attack after hearing about the shooting. Another man was shot and killed, and another was at large. So the level of frustration was increasing by the second. Prior to this, the leads they had were questionable and not convicting. The investigation had come to a screeching halt up to this point. They had a license plate number, but they were unable to find the car to match it. The owner of the car had called the car in stolen shortly after the shooting, and couldn't provide any information that would lead to the second suspect.

"Thanks to the high quality of the video, Cylabs was able to use modern facial recognition software to generate sixty to seventy pixels between the suspects' eyes and apply super-resolution algorithm to the image to

extrapolate what the suspect looks like from straight on."
Detective Gordy explained to Lt. Combs.

Lt. Combs shook his head with approval.

"Then we posted that image online, and within
minutes' leads started pouring in." Detective Gordy
continued saying.

The software she spoke about was created by Mario
Savvides, the head of Carnegie Mellon's Cylab. Using his
software, they were able to generate a 3D version of the
suspect's face from a 2D image. Then they got the public
involved using social media.

"This is excellent work...Excellent work,
guys...Have we located the suspect yet?" Lt. Combs asked.

"We're pursuing a couple of leads."

"Well, for Christ sakes, what the hell are you guys
doin' still standing here? Go get this muthafucka off the
streets!"

COPS & BALLERS II

CRIMINAL COMPLAINT: Case #1220

After a three-hour stand-off in the Lawrenceville section of Pittsburgh, SWAT officers entered a house on 28th St., and arrested Andrew Kaus, 26, of Wilkinsburg, PA., after receiving a tip that the suspect was being held up there. Kaus was charged with the robbery and the shooting of reality TV star, Sexy Duvall, 35. Kaus' accomplice, Brian Clurman, 22, was shot and killed by Duvall during the crime.

Kaus accused his deceased partner of planning the robbery, and the shooting of Duvall. Congruent to the police reports, Kaus is charged with Murder, Robbery, Conspiracy, and Firearm violations. According to court dockets, the two men had discussed robbing Duvall after witnessing her make a large substantial amount of money dancing at club Reflections. Kaus called Duvall in expectations that they were to have sex for money.

Cell phone records indicate that the last call Duvall received came from Kaus' cell phone, which was later found on his person at the time of his arrest.

During interviews with Allegheny County Robbery detectives, Kaus said that Clurman shot Duvall multiple times. And after witnessing his accomplice, Clurman, being shot and killed, Kaus said he got scared and fled the scene. But not before his car was struck by the shooting victim, Sexy Duvall. His statement was reconfirmed by surveillance footage and forensic evidence which shows that on Thursday, April 7, 2016, the two co-conspirators pulled in front of Duvall's car. Blocking her exit, the two men then stepped from the shadows of their car with their weapons drawn. At an extremely close range, Clurman aimed his pistol at Sexy Duvall, who sat behind the steering wheel of her Aston Martin Vanquish and shot into the windshield, driver's side door and window, hitting Duvall five times leaving her engulfed in a rain of lead and broken glass. Duvall was struck in the face, neck, chest, leg and abdomen. Slumped over in her seat, her body riddled with bullets, Duvall waited for the shooter to open her door in attempts to rob her, and when he did, Duvall returned fire shooting through her Barkin bag, hitting the assailant twice, making him stumble backwards, collapse and die. As the second assailant tried to get away, Duvall, found the strength to ram the back of his vehicle in attempts to stop him from escaping.

A quarter of a block away, the gunfire and the car crash was heard by a pedestrian that happened to be driving by at the time of the crime being committed. Seconds later his eyes met those of the fleeing suspect, Andrew Kaus. Focusing on the license plate of the crashed white Dodge Charger, that abruptly pulled out in front of him, he thumbed it into his smart phone. Seeing the direction, the suspect came from, the pedestrian dialed 9-1-1, and headed to where he believed the crime had been committed. After driving for approximately thirty seconds, he came upon a woman later identified as Sexy Duvall lying flat on the street, several feet from her car, court documents state. Kaus was arraigned Wednesday, April 13, 2016, and is being held at the Allegheny County Jail.

"It's a miracle she survived," Monte Bucks said, sitting with one of the producers from the show. After he read over the report he requested. "So what are they doing with her?" He asked about Sexy Duvall, adjusting himself in the leather seat of his home theater.

"Well, she's being charged with a Firearm Violation, the gun she had was stolen. They dropped the manslaughter charge after reviewing the tape cause it's obvious that she was protecting herself."

"Okay, cool. What about bail?"

"The bail situation is difficult because of her condition. They can't remove her from her hospital bed. And like you already know, she's under heavy guard. You saw how much red tape we had to go through to get footage for the Teaser."

"Hey, listen...Call my lawyer. Have him contact the judge and do a bail hearing without her. Get her out and keep her guarded. Pay for twenty-four-hour security just in case these creeps try some other shit, and let's get her on the camera. We need access to her. I'm not paying her all that money for nothing.

"Okay, I'm on it."

***

Mr. Frosty made his way to Platinum Beats, a studio owned by super-producer, Boom Bap. He had an appointment with her that was to be recorded by Love & Trap Muzik, Pittsburgh. But recording a reality show and living a reality show were two different things. So on his way to the recording lab he kept his head on swivel; keeping his eyes opened for any drama life might bring him. Because he knew anything could jump off whether they were recording or not. They had made arrangements for him and the famous producer to meet, but he stayed ready for the unscripted to happen.

Driving through the city of Pittsburgh he had gotten a lot of attention because of the car he was driving, and he knew somewhere in the crowd of onlooker's jealousy and jackers were lurking. Platinum records, money, jewelry, and cars were just an attraction that could lead to trouble sometimes even death, and he possessed them all.

Mr. Frosty Blow was a real street nigga that came from the hood, and had put in work growing up in the hood. The street element of the city knew this so whenever he brought out his toys, jackers thought twice about trying him. Mr. Frosty wasn't the type of rapper just rapping about shit he didn't live, he lived the shit he rapped about. Anyone stepping up to test him knew that there would be consequences and repercussions about fucking with his.

Unlike his rival, Smack Down, he rarely traveled in a pack unless he was traveling with his business associates. He was licensed to carry and stayed strapped with his FN Herstatal 5.7 tactical pistol. It held twenty in the clip, one in the chamber, fired high velocity rounds, and penetrated bullet proof vest.

For the Teaser Party, he chose to ride in his brand new, straight off the lot, red Lambo' Truck, but for the show he decided to pull out his '73 Chevy Caprice Donk on 10.5-inch wide wheels. Its engine was transformed into a 632ci BBC dyno-ed at 905hp on pump gas with no power adders or nitrous. It was the most powerful heart you could put in a Donk. Everything about his Caprice said money, even his break system had cost him over eight stacks.

Platinum Beats was located on the twenty-fifth floor of PNC Plaza, a condo building in downtown Pittsburgh's hottest new district, adjacent to the thriving new development of Market Square, and a burgeoning retail and restaurant scene. The six-bedroom duplex penthouse were converted into Studio Room's A, B, C, D, E and F. It's original structural columns and beam ceilings, sprawled across 4,500 square foot on two levels with more than 3,000 square-feet of open loft living that served as an outdoor dining area complete with waiters and barmaids. A cantilevered solid oak and steel staircase called "Boom Bap's Ladder," ascended to the twenty-sixth floor or as Boom Bap called it "Heaven", where everything was white including the furniture, appliances, everything in her master suite and living space of eleven foot, six-inch ceilings, dressing room, bath, and kitchenette that came with a personal chef and living room. Floor to ceiling windows slid open to a roomy terrace with a stone patio and a hot tub.

On this day, Boom Bap's sessions were running close. At the last moment she had decided to squeeze a client in between her meeting with Mr. Frosty Blow. The Love & Trap Muzik, Pittsburgh camera crew dined on the patio while she handled some last minute business, while they waited for Mr. Frosty Blow to arrive.

"Come on...You gotta hurry up and cum...Come on," Boom Bap said, eating her client's pussy. She had snuck her into Studio F without the camera crew knowing.

"Mmm mmm," she moaned as she fucked her client with an eleven-inch dildo, kissing her. Boom Bap was forty-five and had a thing for young boys, as well as younger women between the ages of twenty and twenty-five years old. The real reason she was mad at producer Making Hitz wasn't because he went into business for himself, she was proud of him for that. It was because he had cut her off and had stopped fucking her. The night of the Teaser Party she watched him all night long mingle with different woman, including Beyoncé and Nicki Minaj. "That young nigga gotta big ass dick, and he can fuck," she told her girls talking about Making Hitz.

***

Mr. Frosty Blow made his way through the lobby lounge of Platinum Beats Studio, and asked the receptionist to let Boom Bap and the camera crew know that he was there.

"Okay, I'll let 'em know." She told him as he took a seat on one of the plush chairs in the lobby lounge area, looking out the wall of windows permitting a panoramic scene of downtown Pittsburgh. Instead of literature, iPads covered the table in the waiting room. At one click of your finger you could access any book or magazine of your preference. He stood up and looked over at people walking through Market Square as the camera crew began to walk into the lobby.

***

"Nnnn...Nnnn...Nnn," Boom Bap's cell phone vibrated. "You came just in time, baby." She told her client as they adjusted their clothes. Bap answered her phone. "Yea, I'm coming out now." Boom Bap told her receptionist.

"How I look?" Boom Bap's client asked.

"Like you just got ya pussy ate."

"Ha ha, bitch you crazy."

"Nah, you straight. You ready?" Boom Bap asked with her hand on the door knob ready to exit the recording room.

When they entered the room Boom Bap's client spoke. "Mr. Frosty Blow, what's up, baby?"

"America, what you doin' here?" Mr. Frosty Blow asked Boom Bap's secret client.

"America, are you taping too?" The cameraman asked. "You may as well, America. I mean if it's okay wit' you, Frosty."

Mr. Frosty Blow thought about it. "I mean she can stay if she try'na do ah collabo'." He said with a smile on his face.

"I'm wit' it. I need that platinum touch to rub off on me," America replied.

"There it is. Mic us up." Boom Bap told the camera crew.

ACTS OF WAR

"Smack, check dis bitch out." Hitter B, showed Smack Down an *Instagram* picture of America and Mr. Frosty Blow, posted up together at Platinum Beats Studio. The caption below the picture read, "At the studio with Platinum Beat Maker, Boom Bap, and the owner of Pittsburgh's streets."

"Get da fuck outta here. Dat nigga don't own the streets, we do! Bitch crrrazy!" Smack Down was tight about what he read, his gaze was firmly planted on the screen of Hitter B's smart phone.

"Bra, it's time to repo our streets from dat nigga, and jack dat bitch. You know I just got that new spot. It's outta the way. We can take that bitch there, and make her tell us where all that money is." Hitter B tried to convince Smack Down to kill Mr. Frosty Blow, and kidnap America.

"Be easy, homie. They down there on camera. But we gon' go holla at dat nigga, though. I'm tired of that muthafucka acting like he owns shit. This my muthafuckin' city, our muthafuckin' city!"

"You fuckin' right it is, Smack." Hitter B said, and the rest of the Smack Dizzy Boys bobble headed in agreement.

"Y'all niggas stay here, and put this work together. Me and Hitter gon' go holla at dat nigga. Break these four birds down in quarter bricks, double these three, and put these three up." Smack Down told his crew, taking his Walther PPX .40 Caliber out of his waist band. He ejected the clip, made sure it was fully loaded, inserted it back in, slid the slide back and loaded one into the chamber.

"Yo Earn', don't go down there doin' shit on camera. Smack man, we got a lot ridin' on you. You don't need no case." Smack Down's second in charge, Cash and No Non-Sense, told him.

"Nigga, shut da fuck up wit' dat scared shit. Dat nigga out here disrespectin', and you scared to catch ah case."

"You shut da fuck up!" Smack Down's second in charge said, standing up ready to rumble if he had to.

"You right, CNN, we gotta watch out for shit like dis. We can't afford to get indicted on gun charges, drug charges, or none of dat shit."

***

Coming out of Platinum Beats Studio at 3:47 A.M., America and Mr. Frosty Blow talked about their collaboration track. They put together a song called, "Likin' Her". On it America rapped, and Mr. Frosty Blow sung the hook.

"This was supposed to be my session, my song. I don't know how I let you take over my session. We was supposed to be workin' on ah song for my album," Mr. Frosty Blow said, slowly shaking his head with a childish smile on his face.

The camera crew was still recording the two artists for the show. The Love & Trap Muzik, Pittsburgh's security stood by. They were always on duty when it came to recording for the show.

Suddenly a Beleza Edition Mercedes-Benz Sprinter pulled up, and Dominican Flames and her people poured out. Security stood by while the camera crew kept recording. Monte Bucks had arranged for the confrontation to happen. He wanted to capture America and Dominican Flames' beef on tape. He knew that Dominican Flames was upset about her footage getting leaked.

"There they go right there, Smack. All lovey-dovey an' shit." Hitter B and Smack Down had pulled up and parked outside of Platinum Beats Studio, seconds before Dominican Flames had jumped out on America.

"Nigga, boll up. You don't see security?" Smack Down asked Hitter B, stopping him from exiting the car. "I ain't try'na catch ah Fed case 'bout no stupid shit."

"OH SHIT! LOOK, SMACK! Hitter B said, pointing towards Dominican Flames jumping out on America and Mr. Frosty Blow.

"Bitch, how da fuck you playin' me. I do all dat shit fa' you and ya moms, and you cross me! Who da fuck gave you my footage?!" Dominican Flames yelled, giving America an icy look, balling her fist up.

91

"What?! Get da fuck outta here wit' dat shit!" America yelled back.

"Hol' up...Hol' up!" Mr. Frosty Blow stood between the two angry females.

"Nigga, you betta get da fuck out the way! Dis between me and dat snake ass bitch! You ain't got nothin' to do with dis!" Dominican Flames yelled at Mr. Frosty Blow.

"Nah, fam, you hold up!" One of Dominican Flames' henchmen said, stepping towards Mr. Frosty Blow.

"Look at dat nigga, Smack. He bitchin' up." Hitter B said as him and Smack Down watched from the car.

"You don't want dis, you really don't! Believe me!" Mr. Frosty said with his mind on the strap he was carrying.

"Why don't I, nigga?!"

"Bitch!" America swung on Dominican Flames.

"Bitch, take my footage..."

"Get da fuck..."

"Yo! Yo! Stop!"

Dominican Flames grabbed a hand full of America's hair. They started scuffling. Before Mr. Frosty Blow and Dominican Flames' henchmen could get into it security intervened.

"Pull off, nigga," Smack Down told Hitter B.

"Hm?" Hitter B wanted to get involved in the drama.

"Yo, dawg, pull off...Pull da fuck off! Police about to be down at dis bitch. We downtown Pittsburgh," Smack Down said.

***

Two days before the America versus Dominican Flames confrontation, America and her brother, Ran, sat at their mother's stunning stone home nestled on a 6.2-acre tabletop lot in Fox Chapel, listening to some tracks Boom Bap had emailed to America.

"Dat shit's hard right there," Ren said bobbing his head to a Drake styled beat.

"You like dat?" America asked mentally fitting her lyrics to the track. She started flowing under her breath. Bobbing her head and motioning her hands in the air, when her cell phone rung. "Hello

"Turn to Channel 0 News, Ren. They caught dat dude!"

"Thank you, auntie...I'ma hit you right back." Their aunt had called to let them know that the second suspect in their mother's shooting had been caught.

CHANNEL 0 NEWS: "Stand Off Ends In Man's Arrest," The headline read at the bottom of the screen.

"A suspect in the reality star shooting was held up in an apartment for three hours before surrendering. A little before four P.M., SWAT officers entered the house on 28th St., and arrested the only occupant, Andrew Kaus, 28, from Homewood, more than three hours after the stand-off

began. The incident started about 1:00 P.M., after police received an anonymous call about the shooting suspects whereabouts, authorities said. When Firefighters arrived, the suspect threatened them, police were threatened, and that's when Kaus displayed his gun through the downstairs window.

Police then spent more than three hours trying to get Kaus to come out, hailing him with a loudspeaker, urging him to come out of the house. When he did not cooperate SWAT officers threw canisters of tear gas into the house, and drove the suspect to surrender.

That's the latest, reporting live from Lawrenceville, Guy Speaks, Channel 0 News."

"You got this?" America asked Ren.

"All over it, sis'," Ren said, thumbing a number into his cell phone.

***

"See now, there's a huge misconception about black guys and big dicks. I done stripped searched thousands of these fuckas and only eight out of ten of 'em got big dicks. I gotta bigger dick than some of these ma'fuckas. Some of the black guys I've stripped searched I've given an apology because their dicks are an embarrassment to the black race...Ha ha ha." C.O. Gene Hooker entertained his wife during dinner at their Sewickly home.

"Ha ha ha, Gene!"

His phone rung. "Oh, hol' up, babe. I gotta take this call." Stepping away from the dinner table, C.O. Hooker took a call from Ren. "'Sup, brotha...No, I haven't seen it...You got it...Ha, that's what I'm talkin' 'bout...Soon as I can...Aight...I'm back, babe." C.O. Hooker said taking his seat at the dinner table.

"Gene, I don't wanna hear no more about black guy's dicks, ha ha." C.O. Hooker's wife was enjoying her husband's company. He had an hour before he had to go in to work, and they spent it having dinner. C.O. Hooker worked the 11-7 A.M. shift, so she always cooked dinner, and they sat and ate together before he went in.

Gene and Ren grew up together and played football together. But now they were crime partners. With the help of Gene, Ren flooded the prison system with cell phones and drugs. One forty-dollar cell phone sold for twenty-five hundred dollars in some jails, and they made ten times as much off of drugs as would a drug dealer selling them in the streets.

Ren was calling for a favor, and Gene liked doing favors for Ren because they paid off well.

***

The night of the America vs Dominican Flames beef, America and Mr. Frosty ate breakfast at Bob Evans.

"Yea, dat bitch rolled up on me coming out of the studio an' shit...Nah, I'm cool, I'm with Frosty...Cool, I'll see you when I get home." America had called her brother and told him about what had happened outside of Platinum Beats Studio.

***

Home studio on the Northside...

Lied to my man, said I was ten minutes away/

but I'm at the spot, whippin' ah half ah brick of yay/

choppa on the table, got two pits at the door/

nina on my navel, half ah brick on the floor...

As Blocks N Bricks recorded a song for his mixtape at a home studio on the Northside of Pittsburgh, the streets were brewing with beef. The cast of Love & Trap Muzik, Pittsburgh, was about to give the world a show they would never forget.

***

After Ren heard about Dominican Flames stepping to his sister, he felt that he had to take action. Dressed in all black he drove to club Reflections during closing. He wanted to go into the club, and shoot it up, but when he pulled up there were police and security all over the place. They were waiting to get paid, they always got paid at the end of their shift. Ren, even saw the Love & Trap Muzik, Pittsburgh's camera crew lurking around, so this meant not only was he taking a risk of being caught on the club's security cameras, he was taking a risk of being recorded by the show. So he kept it moving, but he didn't have any intensions of letting things go.

Driving back home he thought about how reckless he was thinking. He thought about the footage his sister had brought, and thought

that the same security cameras that led to his mother's shooter's capture could have led to his. Then he found an angle. He would get at the security that had sold his sister the footage, and pay him for Dominican Flames' home address. He wanted to send his boss, Dominican Flames a message.

Taking his cell phone out of the cup holder of his mother's Vanquish, he thumbed America's number into it, and pressed send to call her. After a few rings she answered.

"'Sup brother?"

"Text me that security guard's number, I need to get at him," Ren told his sister.

"What security guard?"

99

Mr. Frosty looked up at America, putting a tip on the table at Bob Evans. He wondered who she was talking to.

"The one that had the footage," Ren said.

"Aight got you. Be careful, brother." America told her only sibling.

A few minutes later the security guards number popped up in Ren's message box: Pedro 412-777-8888.

***

"Bandana on my face, I took ah hammer to the cake/ Peruvian flake, it's that scaley white product/smashed it into powder, heated that Vision Ware pot up..."

As the engineer watched Blocks N Bricks spit his lyric's, he adjusted his vocals on the mixing board as the Love & Trap Muzik, Pittsburgh, camera crew recorded the session.

***

I Need A Bawss In My Life

On the other side of town, Ren met with Pedro. In exchange for five-thousand dollars, he provided Ren with Dominican Flames' address.

"Now step back." Ren told Pedro, walking up to the Mercedes-Benz Sprinter with his AR-I5 in hand

"Hol' up!" Pedro tried to stop Ren.

"Look fam', this bitch can get shot up by itself, or you can get shot up wit' it." Ren gave Pedro a menacing look, letting him know how serious he was about what he was saying. And without hesitation, Pedro stepped to the side.

Ren lifted his AR-15, and started popping shots at the Sprinter. "Rrrrraaaat-ah-tat tat tat...BURSHH! Rrrat-ah-tat tat...POP! Rrrat-ah-tat tat tat...POOF!" Ren shot holes into the Mercedes-Benz Sprinter customized by Lexani Motorcars, shot out its windows, its body, tires, and destroyed the 48" curved 4k VHD TV and other electronics inside of it.

***

At the Allegheny County Jail at 3:18 A.M., C.O. Hooker popped cell one in Unit 6D.

Hearing his cell door being popped, Andrew Kaus opened his eyes. "Man, what da fuck!" He said, feeling irritated. "I don't feel like answering no mo' fuckin' questions. I told these muthafuckas everything." Andrew Kaus believed that he was being pulled out of his cell by federal agents to answer more questions about the Sexy Duvall case. But before he could sit up and gather himself, C.O. Hooker was standing over him.

"Stand up, and turn around." C.O. Hooker told him firmly.

"Man, what da..."

"Stand up, and turn around, NOW!"

"This is crazy," Andrew Kaus said turning around and before he could say another word, C.O. Hooker put him in a choke hold.

***

Home Studio

...Let it cook ah wit' da fire on medium/

*grabbed the squirt gun, and wit' da water started squeezin'
it/*

took ah butterknife, and I slowly started whipping

In ah couple minutes, the coc' started lookin' different...

Allegheny Jail

"Mm...Mm...Mmmm...Wha...Wha..." Andrew Kaus struggled for his life. "Ssshhh...Shut da fuck up...Shut da fuck up..." C.O. Hooker tightened his grip around Andrew Kaus' neck.

Home Studio

...Went from ah powder to ah paste within' seconds/

strapped down to my beater cause it's hot up in da kitchen/

103

turned da fire off, and I counter topped my weapon...

stripped down to my beater,

cause it's hot up in da kitchen/ turned da fire off,

and I counter topped my weapon/ placed it in ice water,

and I watched it start to harden/ put it on paper towel,

to absorb the water/ let it dry ah li'l,

and I weighed it on my scale/ called back some fiends,

and said, I got this rock for sale/

called back my man, and told him I was on my way,

cause this is how we do it in the cities of P-A...

The engineer stopped the track after he played the verse back.

"You like dat?" Blocks N Bricks asked.

"You gon' have the streets sown up wit' dat shit, straight up."

Allegheny County Jail

"'...Just go out, muthafucka...This is for Sexy...The Duvall family ...I'ma send you to be wit'cha homie...I'ma send you to meet'cha maker, muthafucka." C.O. Hooker said, in a deadly whisper, choking the life out of Andrew Kaus. After a few minutes, Andrew Kaus stopped struggling. Squatting down on the floor of the cell with Andrew Kaus, leaning back on his 6'5" 298-pound body, C.O. Hooker placed one hand on the back of Andrew Kaus' head, and his other at the base of his chin. "CRRRACK," and snapped his neck. Then he dragged his body and leaned it against his bunk.

Home Studio

...Placed it in ice water, and I watched it start to hardened/

put it on paper towel,

to absorbed the water...

Allegheny County Jail

After leaning Andrew Kaus' body against his bunk, C.O. Hooker removed the sheet from his bed, and tore a long strip from it, and tied it into a noose. After tying it to the top bunk, he hoisted Andrew Kaus' neck into its loop, and let his body drop into it.

"Damn!" C.O. Hooker was offended by the stench that started filling the small cell, Andrew Kaus, pissed and shitted himself.

Standing back, C.O. Hooker thoroughly looked over the crime scene, and then he called for help, "Bleep-bleep, we need ah medic in 6D... Please hurry, we need ah medic in 6D."

Home Studio

...Let it dry ah and I weighed it on my scale/

called back some fiends, and said I got this rock fo' sale/

called back my man, and told him I was on my way/

cause this is how we do it in the cities of P.A.

"Play that back," Blocks N Bricks told the engineer, Josh. Taking of his headphones, he sat them down, exited the booth, and entered the engineering room.

"Okay, here we go, Blocks..."

...Lied to my man, said I was ten minutes away/

but I'm at the spot whippin' ah half ah brick of yay/

choppa on the table, got two pits at the door/

nina on my navel, half ah brick on the floor/

bandana on my face, I took ah hammer to the cake/

Peruvian flake, it's that scaley white product/

smashed it into powder, heated dat Vision Ware pot up/

let it cook ah wit' dat fire on medium/

grabbed the squirt gun, and wit' the water, started squeezin' it/

took ah butterknife, and I slowly started whippin'/

in ah couple minutes, the coc' started lookin' different/

went from ah powder to ah paste within seconds/

FRIEND TURNED FOE

Before they were rappers with national notoriety, before they were known as Mr. Frosty Blow and Smack Down, they knew each other as Juwan "Mr. Frosty Blow" King and Taelor "Smack Down" Peterson.

Juwan King and one of his homies sat on his CLS, outside of Langley High school, waiting for his little sister, Money King, to get out of school.

"Aye, ain't you from Northview, yo?" Taelor Peterson asked.

"Why li'l nigga? What the fuck you askin' me questions fo'?! I don't know you," Juwan King asked coldly.

"I know li'l nigga. He from the Heights." Juwan's homie said.

"I neva seen this nigga," Juwan responded looking Taelor up and down. In his Rock-a-Wear sweat suit, iced out necklace, watch and bracelet.

109

"That's Chilli's son." Juwan's homie said, shaking his head up-and-down, as if he was confirming the fact with himself.

"Oh, Chilli's ya mom's?"

"Yea, she my ma. Hey though, I'm try'na get wit' you. I be seein' you doin' ya thing, I gotta couple dollars," Taelor said to Juwan.

"What's ah couple dollars?" Juwan asked curious to find out what the young hustler was working with.

"'Bout fifteen stacks." Taelor told his small audience.

"Oh yea, what you try'na do wit' dat?" Juwan asked.

"Whateva you can do you know?"

"Taelor, what you talkin' to my brotha 'bout?" Money King walked up to the circle of hustlers and asked.

"Oh, you know him too, Money?" Juwan asked his little sister.

"Yea, his crazy butt's in my class. But he barely come to school so caught up hustlin' like you." Money said with an expression of disgust on her face.

"Shut da fuck up!" Juwan told his little sister. "Yo, get in da car I'ma drop you off." He said to Taelor, getting into his luxury car.

"He ain't ridin' wit' us!" Money said as she got in her brother's CLS.

"I said shut da fuck up, Money. Get in li'l homie," Juwan said.

After dropping his sister off, Juwan, drove Tae to his house.

"Yo, get dat paper together. I'ma send my man back around wit' some'in' fo' you. How long you need to get it together?" Juwan asked Tae.

"I already got it together," Tae answered.

"Aight cool. My man ah be right back wit' dat. Put ya number in his phone," Juwan's homie passed Tae his cell phone.

Twenty minutes later, Juwan's homie pulled up in front of Tae's house, and called him. "I'm out front," he told Tae.

Rushing out of his house, Tae got into Juwan's CLS, and passed his homie a white grocery bag. "Here you go," Tae said.

"Dis fifteen, right?"

"Yea yup. What's dis?"

"It's ah bird. You owe fourteen."

"Okay, no problem."

***

Four months later, in 2003, Tae had been working for a few months. He dropped out of school, but had advanced in his street education. He went from adding up numbers in a text book to adding stacks of money up. From carrying books in backpacks to carrying guns and stacks in his backpacks. From playing ball in gym class to ballin' on the street. From taking Jay's to jackin' hustlers for kilos.

And by this time, Money had caught feelings for him, but he was focused on getting his paper.

At first they were calling each other brother and sister, but Tae started noticing how jealous she got when he would talk to other females around her, and so did her brother, Juwan.

"You gon' have sis' kill one of dem bitches you fuckin' wit'. She's really feelin' you, bro. I knew dat when we first met. "Juwan said, passing Tae a blunt filled with Dro. They were sitting at a table in a trap-house, weighing work up.

"Bro, she's like my sister. Yaw's moms call me her son," Tae replied.

Inhaling Dro smoke into his lungs. It made him cough, forcing him to exhale.

"Yea, like ah son-in-law, homie. Plus, Money ain't try'na hear dat brotha shit! You should take her to ah club or should take her out to eat or to ah movie or some'in." *Juwan suggested.*

A week later, Tae did just that. But his plan was to change her mind about liking him.

"You know this'll neva work, don't you?" Tae said to Money, wiping the smile right off of her face. They were on their way to dinner and a movie.

"We can make it work. You just don't want it to work," Money said.

"Who told you I wanted ah girl in da first place? I don't need no girlfriend."

"You right, you don't need no girlfriend, you need a woman," Money responded to Tae's response.

"Oh, and you da woman I need? You haven't even graduated yet."

"We graduate this year."

"We? I'm not gain' back to school." Tae muttered.

"See, I told you, you need ah woman. YOU-ARE-GOIN'-BACK-TO-SCHOOL! And I'm gonna help you getcha diploma, Tae."

Tae, got quiet and studied the firm expression on Money's face. He was in deep thought. "See Money, that's what I'm talkin' 'bout. See you's ah straight A student, you're good at school. Me, I'ma street nigga."

"You sound stupid, but I know ya not stupid." Money stopped Tae from down grading himself.

"I'm just sayin' Money, you don't need no boyfriend like me, I ain't no good fo' you. Niggas like me go to jail fo' ah very long time, or end up dead. I've accepted them terms, can you?"

"Mm-hm, I can accept that, but I will not allow either of us to be satisfied wit dat."

"Look Money...You deserve mo'."

"I want you. Look Tae, what I'm sayin' is, I know that those outcomes are inevitable, but you don't have to settle for those two outcomes. As a street person as you call yourself, you actually have a better chance to make something more of yourself. You're out here makin' thousands and thousands of dollars every day. That's not common for a seventeen-year-old. You can take some of

115

that money and invest it. You can use the game as a stepping stone instead of a grave stone."

"Hmph," Tae listened. Money had his attention and was making a lot of sense.

"Instead of makin' thousands, you could make millions the right way. You don't have to die for this, or go to jail, if you plan right. And the only way to plan this right is you gotta go back to school." Money was saying all of the right things.

"See, I don't like nobody try'na change me. Plus, you on some jealous shit. I'm out here livin', I ain't try'na be tied down." Tae's mind scrambled for excuses.

"Whateva Tae! I don't care nothin' 'bout ya li'l bitches. And I ain't try'na tie you down. I just want the best for you."

"And you're the best fo' me?" Tae asked.

"Yes. I am the best for you. Tae, you can do whatever you want. I don't care. Just be there for me when I need you. Put me before all of ya other bitches. When I

call, when I want you, come. I don't care what ya ass is into, or who you wit'."

A week after their date, Tae started going back to school, and for the following   months, Money helped him maintain good grades. He was still seeing other women, so Money decided to play his game. She started dating another baller named Mar Mar.

Mar Mar was a hustler from Garfield. He owned a Salon and a Rib Shack, and drove a Bentley Spur. Seeing this made Tee jealous. Money stopped answering his calls every time he called, and was spending more time with Mar Mar than with him.

***

"Yo, what's up wit' you and dat nigga you been hangin' out wit'?" Tae asked Money in the hallway at school.

"What you meeeaan?"

"You know what I mean, Money."

"Look at you. Now you worried 'bout who I'm seeing. You ain't care before. Plus, you out here fuckin' all these bitches."

"See, here you go. I thought you ain't care."

Money got quiet for a minute. "You know I care."

"If you really fucked wit' me like dat, you'd help me jack dat nigga. I seen him picking you up in ah Bentley. He got a lot of money?" Tae asked.

"Yea, he got a lot of money," Money told Tae.

"You fuckin' dat nigga?"

"NO! I'm not fuckin' nobody. Did I fuck you?"

"Nah. I was just checking to see if you were still ah virgin. I thought he might of popped dat cherry."

"Hmph!" Money crossed her arms across her chest and pouted. She was saving herself for him, and didn't appreciate his disrespectful comments.

"Look, this is what I'll do. If you help me get dat nigga, I'll cut these bitches off and be with you."

"Are you gon' finish school?"

"Yea, as long as you keep helping me," Tae answered.

"Aight. Let me find out where he keeps all his money at. He don't really trust me right now. But Tae, whatever you do, do not kill him. I'm not try'na live with that on my conscience," Money said.

Two weeks before graduation, Mar Mar and Money sat in the food court of Monroeville Mall.

"All this shoppin', when you gon' let me hit some'in'? I've been waitin' fo' ah minute. You know I gotta like you cause I don't play this no sex shit," Mar Mar said to Money.

"I suck ya dick," Money said rolling her eyes and neck.

"Yea, but I'm try'na get some of that pussy. Why you holdin' out?"

"When you learn to trust me is when I'll give you some."

"Trust you? I trust you."

"We've been dating for a few months now, and we still going to hotels. You must have a wife or something."

"Ha ha ha, ah wife. Hell no, you trippin'. I'm try'na make you my wife."

"Yea okay. If you were, I would be going to your house not no hotel every time we hook up."

"You wanna go to my spot? Come on, I'll take you." Mar Mar got up from the dining table and said.

Fifteen minutes later, Mar Mar's Bentley was pulling up at a renovated home that sat on two acres.

"Wow, this is your house?" Money asked. Her eyes lit up at the sight of Mar Mar's mansion.

"Yup. Come on, let me show you the inside."

Soon as they got in the door, Money could hear a group of people talking somewhere in the near distance.

"Dat's my brother, my sister-in-law, and their kids. They come over every weekend just to kick it. And I don't mind cause don't nobody else ever be here. You know? I got four bedrooms, two and a half baths, custom built in media center in the family room, top of the line appliances, so you can cook for me and our kids..."

"Ha ha, yeeeaah?"

"Yup. And I got ah rear hot tub and dipping pool. You know, ah li'l some'in, some'in'. So you ready to step things up? This is just a part of what I have to offer." Mar Mar paused and hugged Money around her waist. "So you ready to be wifey?" He asked.

Money nodded her head. "Yes."

Mar Mar kissed Money. "Dat's what I'm talkin' 'bout. So you ready to see our bedroom?"

"Yea, you can show it to me, but we ain't doing nothing right now," Money firmly stated.

"Come on. Why you still playin'?"

"Be patient. I got you. Just not right now."

***

A week before graduation, Money and Tae watched a movie at Tae's Bellevue spot. Suddenly, Money grabbed Tae's hand and led him into the bedroom. The light from beyond the door created a silhouette of their images, holding each other. Money was ready to give herself to Tae. They were graduating in a week, and Tae had given up all of his side pieces. At least that's what Money believed. So now she wanted to share herself with the only man she had ever loved.

"What?" Tae asked face to face with Money.

Money walked over to the bed, and Tae finally realized what Money's eyes and body language were trying to tell him.

"Oh shit! You...you..."

Money nodded her head yes.

"You sure? I don't want to pressure you."

"Ssshhh." Money put her finger to her mouth to hush Tae.

Tae walked up to Money and pecked her on the lips, the forehead and neck.

Money took Tae's face into both of her hands and kissed him passionately for several seconds. Then she walked sexily to the bedroom dresser, and lit two scented candles. Then she pressed play on an iPod that was cradled on its port, and an Old School Baby Maker mix started playing Jodeci's song Forever My Lady.

...For-ever ...For-ever ...For-ever/ I know ew-ah ..,

So ya havin' my bay -be/

and it means so much to meee-e/ there's nothin' mo' precious/

then to raise ah fam-a-leee ...

Money walked slowly towards Tae, unraveling her paisley-print silk chiffon top. She let it fall to the floor as Jodeci set the mood.

"If there's any doubt in ya mind/ you can count on me"

Watching Money, Tae kicked off his Run-DMC Adidas and loosened the belt holding up his Evisu jeans, never releasing his eyes from Money's 34DD breast contained by her Frederick's of Hollywood bralet.

"I'll neva let you down/lady believe in me"

Grabbing Tee's Adidas Big dot pullover hoodie by its seam, Money helped him lift it over his head and kissed him passionately again.

"You and I (will neva fall apart)

You and I (we knew right from the start)

The day (we fell so far in love)

Now our baby is born so healthy and strong/

now our dreams are reality...

Forever My Lady"

Grabbing Money by her legs, Tae hoisted her up, and Money wrapped her legs around his waist.

"Please, be gentle." Money told Tae.

Tae walked her to the bed and let her fall softly upon it. Sitting on the edge of the bed with Tae standing in front of her, Money wedged his pants down. Tae's erection popped out at her.

"What a pleasant surprise," she said looking at part of Tae's manhood that was partially exposed through the slit of his boxers. Digging his huge pussy-slayer out of its hole, she grabbed Tae by the backside and filled her mouth up with it, taking in as much of it as she could.

Her mouth was warm. She sucked on his dick and licked around the crown of it, looking up at him with her cock-sucking eyes. Tae had his head back, looking upward at the ceiling. "Oooh."

Money's neck pecked back-and-forth, and nice-and-slow. Then Tae looked down at Money as his monstrous pussy-slayer slid in-and-out of her dick eater.

"Oh, no you don't. You ain't makin' me cum," Tae said pulling his dick back from Money's dripping mouth. She scooted forward, wanting it back in the wet warmth of her mouth.

Tae gently pushed Money back onto the bed and pulled her printed boyfriend fit jeans off. Then he slid her thong off as she lifted her buttocks up from king sized mattress, slowly revealing her shaven cunt.

Its lips were fat, her clit stuck out like a sore thumb. Tae turned her over. "What are you doin'?" Money asked.

"Shut up. Just put that ass in the air."

There she sat, in the doggy style position parting her ass cheeks. Tae licked up-and-down her dick gobbling slit. He even tongued her asshole.

"Ew, Tae," Money let out. "Mmm, daddy!" Her muffles unheard due to her face being buried into the pillow. Tae ate her ass and fingered her tight pussy.

"Oooh-aw." She groaned.

"You want me to stop?" Tae asked. Money shook her head, no. Tae continued to maneuver his finger in-and-out of her tight spot trying to force his stiff tongue into her ass.

"Mmm ...Oh ...Tae ...Tae," Money expressed the pleasure she was feeling.

Driving his tongue up the crack of her ass, Tae began to kiss Money's lower back. "Mmuu-ah. Mmuu-ah," he moaned as he was doing it. Money's pussy was dripping wet. Kneeling behind her, Tae took a hold of his ten-and-a-half-inch shaft, and ran it up-and-down Money's drenched cum slit. It sent a tingling sensation up her spine. Then Tae tried to enter her. The tip of his dick was round and wide as a half of a dollar.

"Ou-ah ...Ouu-ah!" Money felt herself being spread open. It hurt a

little, but she didn't want Tae to stop. "You want me to stop?" Tae asked again.

"NO!" Money cried out. "Keep goin'," she told Tae. But Tae stopped

anyway. "What? Why you stop," Money looked back at Tae with her ass in the air, begging to be fucked good.

"Turn over," Tae told her, and Money did as she was told. The piano of Force M.D.'s Tender Love started playing:

"Here I lay all alone/ toss and turning/

long-ing fo' some of your tender love"

Tae took Money's right foot into his hands and began to massage it. Money threw her head back, completely relaxed. Then her head popped up, and her eyes opened widely. The feeling of Tae's soft, wet tongue slipping between each of her toes made her react this way.

"I'm waitin' fo' the right moment to come/

so I can thank you fo'

all the tender love you've given to me"

Money's pussy juices oozed out of her cunt. The clear fluid leak down between her ass cheeks. "Ew, that feels so good, Tae."

Then Tae applied a little pressure to the bottom of her foot and made her toes spread apart. One by one, he sucked her pedicured toes, starting with her big toe.

"Tender love (tender love) Love so tender (ah ...ah ...ah)"

"Mmmm...Ooooh...Tae. Tae, bay-be." Money moaned. Slowly she ran her hand down her tight, six pack abdominal and started rubbing her clit in a circular motion with the middle finger of her right hand.

"That feel good?" Tae stopped licking and sucking her toes to ask.

"Ooh ...Yes, baby ...Yes." Money said slipping her hot pink colored fingertip in and out of her pleasure hole.

"Holdin' you close to me/ bay-be, I sur-render"

129

Kissing up her foot, to her inner thigh until his mouth met the destination of her pulsating pussy. Money fed Tae her pussy juice with her dripping fingers. He licked all over them. Then he pulled back the hood of her clit and used the tip of his tongue to drive her completely insane. Tae's tongue flickered back and forth over her clit. "Oh...Fuck...Fuck...Fuck...FUUUCCCK!" Money had her first orgasm. Seeing her creamy white fluids oozing out of her pussy made Tae really go crazy. Snaking his head wildly, he took two fingers, and plugged her tight hole up with them. Then he moved them in-and-out of her. Money started fucking his fingers harder and faster. She was ready to be fucked.

Her body trembled, her eyes rolled to the back off her head, she bit the bottom of her lip, before she screamed out, "TAAAAAE!" She was having another orgasm. This time her fluid gushed out of her pussy like a running faucet.

"What the fuck! Did you piss?" Tae pulled his head back from her pussy and asked.

Money couldn't say a word. She could barely shake her head, no. "Ah...Ah...No...No...I came." She finally let out.

"Damn, you was squirtin'," Tae said working his fingers back into her pussy. "I want you to do it again. Squirt in my mouth." He told Money. She nodded her head, okay.

Fingering her harder and faster, while licking her clit made Money start to scoot backwards.

"Get back here!" Tae told her before putting her legs on his shoulders. He wrapped his arms around her thighs so she could no longer run from him. But he was eating her pussy so good she couldn't help but to fight. She tried pushing his head away from her pussy, but Tae wanted her to squirt again. "Put it in, Tae. Put it in." Money begged. She couldn't take any more of his head game. It was too good. "PUT IT IN. I'M READY, TAE." She grabbed Tae's head.

"You ready fo' the dick? You sure?"

"Yes," Money said.

Kissing up her body, he could feel her trembling. He took each breast, one by one, and licked her nipples.

"Oh...Oh." Every part of Money's body was sensitive.

Kissing up her neck, Tae took a hold of his dick and ran it up and down the slit of Money's pussy. Even that drove her crazy. Her legs jerked.

Then Tae let his dick go. "You put it in." He told Money looking her in the face.

She felt exhausted. Her eyes were slanted, her was body covered in her sweat, and her pussy dripped creamy cum.

Taking a hold of Tae's ten and a half inch, throbbing cock, she positioned

it to enter her hole. Cautiously, Tae eased the tip of his dick into her. "Ouuu-ah...Ou-ah. Don't stop...Don't stop, put it all in me...Do it slow...Do it slow." Money told Tae. Her pussy was a very tight fit for Tae's large Python-like prick. "Mmmm," Money groaned. "I want you to fuck this pussy real good. Fuck it for the first time, really good. Fuck me real good, 'kay Tae?"

"Okay," Tae answered easing his dick into her inch by inch only stopping when he felt Money's finger tips claw into his back. "Aye! Yo!"

"Sorry, baby."

Tae starting working his hips back and forth, in and out of her opening her up more and more.

"Taaae," she whined, but it was what she wanted.

"Get on top," Tae told Money.

"I don't know how to."

"Just get on top of me, and put it in," Tae said getting on his back.

Money climbed on top of him and eased Tae's dick back into her a few inches. Tae took a hold of her hips and forced a few more inches of himself into her. "Go down on it," he told her as he popped his hips driving his dick into her as if he was trying to knock down a wall. Money's body jerked as did his.

Tae grabbed her and flipped her back onto her back with his dick still in her.

"Ooh," Money moaned.

"Sshh." Now it was Tae telling her to hush.

Money grabbed Tae around his hips. She wanted more of him inside of her. "Do it harder," Money told Tae.

"Mm...Mmm...Mm." Tae had his arms braced on the outside of her, lifting himself up as they look down, and watched his dick going in and out of her. "MMM-HM, yesss, harder! Harder."

"Mm...Mm...Mmm." Tae pounded.

"Oouu-aaah...Mm...Mm...Harder, baby. Harrrrd-urrr."

"MM...MM...MM. Tear dis pussy up...Tear dis pussy up. I'ma tear dis pussy up!"

"YES! YES! Daddy, tear it up! Tear it up. Cum in me…Cum in me!"

"Turn over. I want it from the back." Tae said flipping Money over. Then he guided his dick into her hot spot like a heat seeking missile. His plans were to be gentle at first, but Money wanted him to punish her.

Reaching his arm around to the front of Money, Tae fingered her clit while still fucking her from the back.

"Ew-Oh yesss!" Money loudly moaned.

Tae's hips thrusted with more and more momentum. Money turned her head, and her and Tae kissed. The position was awkward, but felt so good to both of them.

"Faster …Harder!" Money demanded making Tae force more of himself into her. As more and more of his thick slab of meat jammed into her pretty tight hole, the more Money gasped for her breath. Then Tae felt a wetness seep out of her pussy. The more he thrusted, the more he felt the wetness cover his lower stomach.

"Oooh…Taaae…My god!" She cried out.

"Damn, dat pussy so wet." Tae said grabbing Money by the hips and driving her face into the pillow. With each thrust he punished and violated her virgin hole. Clawing his hands into Money's 34DD-24-41 frame, he worked a rhythm that made him feel like he was about to cum.

Money's head tossed back and forth with each stroke. She moaned and begged him not to stop. Tears streamed from her eyes from the pleasure.

"SMACK! You like that? SMACK! You like that?"

"Yes...yes, baby. Smack that ass...Smack it!"

"SMACK!" Tae smacked Money's ass again. Money started throwing her ass back at Tae.

"Yes...Yes, Tae. Yes." Money screamed in pleasure throwing her ass backwards with more force. Driving his lengthy rod into her until his balls slapped and banged off of the thickness of her mischievous beaver. Tae slid it out, gradually, before pounding it again.

"Oh…oh…oh…oh!" Money felt every inch of him. Clinching the sheets with both hands, she tried to brace herself. But Tae pound her pussy until she laid flat on the be, and kept pounding her pussy. "You-want-this-pussy-beat-up, huh?"

"Mm, yes…Mm, yes! Tae…Tae…Taaae," she cried her lover's name out as she experienced her third orgasm. "I'm cummin'…I'm cummin'…"

"Oooooh, shiiiit! I…I…Um…I'm…Meeee toooo, baaay!"

They came at the same time.

"Yoooo," Tae yelled. His ass cheeks clinched together again and again as he shot hot, sizzling cum into Money's insides.

Money's body quivered and her knees got weak. She couldn't withstand the weight of Tae. She collapsed as she came. Tae fell on top of her and rolled over to the side. They both panted, but were without words and energy. Feeling the wetness of Money's body, Tae reached down for himself.

"Daamn bae." He said looking over at Money. He tried to scoot up on her to hold her.

"No...Don't...Touch...Ah...Ah...touch me." She was sensitive to his every touch. She just wanted to lay there for a minute, until what she was feeling was over.

Tae backed away from her and reached down for himself again. "Something ain't right!"

"What you meeeaaan?" Money turned over and asked.

"Yo," Tae sniffed his fingers. *"Yo! I think you're bleedin' or somethin',"* Tae said.

"WHAT?" Money got up and ran to the light switch and turned it on. *"Ewwww!"* She turned the lights back out. *"I'm sooo fuckin' embarrassed. I must be spotting."* She said running to the bathroom.

What neither of the two inexperienced lovers knew was Tae had popped Money's cherry.

Mar Mar had finally slipped and was overheard talking business over the phone. Money had spent close to forty minutes sucking his dick and swallowing his cum. She had put him to sleep.

At around 3:00 A.M., they both were awakened by his cell phone ringing. But Money pretended to still be sleep.

Mar Mar, stepped into the hallway to take the call. "You want me to meet you somewhere, or are you going to come to the crib again?" Money overheard him saying. "Cool. You gon' bring it here...Aight, tomorrow night at ten."

"This could be big. I gotta tell Tae," Money thought to herself, still lying lifeless in the bed, faking a light snore until Mar Mar got back into the bed and wrapped his arms around her.

"Mm, you okay, baby?" Money asked.

"Yea. That was my man. I got something to do tomorrow. I might need ya help," Mar Mar told Money.

Normally, he used his brother's wife to take his work to his stash spot, but now that Money had earned his trust, he wanted to start using her. He had purposely left large sums of money lying around her, and she never asked for a dollar or took any of it. To him that proved that she was not a money hungry bitch, and Mar Mar liked that.

"Tomorrow's gon' be ah special night. You should make it better by giving me some of that pussy." Mar Mar said.

"I was thinking the same thing. I think I'm ready for that dick. You've been good to me." Money told him, lying.

"Worrrd?! Come on. We should get it poppin' now."

"No bay. Not now. I'm tired. I got you after you handle ya business. I promise."

"You promise?" Mar Mar asked with a smile on his face. He was happy that he was finally going to have sex with Money. Her head game was bomb, but he wanted to fuck her. Maybe even get her pregnant.

"Yes. I promise, babe. Now let's go back to sleep," Money said clasping her hands over his.

"That's what I'm talkin' 'bout. Hey, tomorrow I'ma need you to drive somethin' somewhere." Mar Mar told Money.

"Okay, babe. Whatever you want, I got you." Money said.

Mar Mar kissed the back of Money's head. He loved how down she was.

The day of the jack, Tae knew that he would need help. Money being caught up in the middle of the jack meant he couldn't ask her brother for help. Juwan would never approve of his sister being used as bait, so Tae called his friend, CNN. He was a wild nigga from the Heights that moved work for him.

The day after Mar Mar had took Money to his estate, she had told Tae where he lived and how the inside was laid out. So he was familiar with the Township. The thing that really concerned Tae was the cops that patrolled that area.

AT 9:00 P.M., Tae and CNN put one in the air, listening to Project Pat's Layin' Da Smack Down, while they were on the way to do the jack.

"Look nigga, no matter what happens don't kill nobody. We goin' to get dat money and Money is up there too, so be careful." Tae told CNN.

"Money's up there?" CNN asked in disbelief. "Yea. This her move."

"Whaaat?! Get the fuck outta here, not school girl."

"Hell yea."

"Oh, that's why Frosty ain't here wit' us." CNN said.

Due to Juwan flooding the streets with blow and he was draped in over a hundred thousand dollars' worth of iced out jewelry, he started calling himself, Mr. Frosty Blow.

"Frosty can't know about this. You feel me?" Tae said to CNN.

"I got you. But how we gon' do this?" CNN asked.

"Look, dude got a nice li'l wooded area around his spot. We gon' park and make our why through da woods up to his spot. Lay there till we see some'in', then move. Soon as homie pull up wit' the work, we jump out on they ass" Tae said taking the blunt from CNN and hitting it. "Money got her ears open. Soon as she hears some'in', she gon text me."

"How many niggas we talkin' 'bout?" CNN asked.

"I ain't sure. Dat's why we got ta hit 'em wit' the element of surprise, and lay they asses down quickly! But if it's too many niggas we just gon' fall back fo' ah minute."

10:30 P.M.

"What da fuck, bruh?! It's like 10:30," CNN whispered as they watched Mar Mar's driveway through the darkness of the woods that surrounded his luxurious estate.

"Hol' up, dis Money right here." Tae pressed the button on his cell phone's ear piece. *"Yo! We right outside,"* Tae told Money. He was crouched down behind some trees. He had butterflies and his stomach was turning. Adrenaline pumped through his veins. *"Okay."* Tae hung up with Money. *"Click-Clack, dude 'bout to pull up now."* He told CNN, cocking his strap back. Money had called and put him on point.

"CLICK-CLACK!" CNN cocked the slide back on his weapon also. They pulled their mask over their faces and waited.

"We should try to go get up under that niggas whip." CNN said observing Mar Mar's Bentley in the driveway.

"Naw. It's too late, too risky. Dat nigga might got cameras. He might be watchin'," Tae told CNN.

Two minutes later, a Kia Sedona pulled into Mar Mar's driveway.

"Let' get it." CNN was ready to move out, but Tae stopped him.

"No C', wait fo' dude to come out." Tae wanted to wait till Mar Mar came out to meet his plug before they moved out.

A few seconds later, Mar Mar did just that. "Hey bruh, what up…"

"PUT YA HANDS UP…PUT YA HANDS UP MUTHAFUCKAS!" CNN and Tae came out of the bushes yelling.

"Nigga, stop runnin' fo' I fill ya ass up wit' dis lead!" CNN let off a warning shot, stopping Mar Mar in his tracks. Seeing two masked men emerge from the woods spooked him and made him try to run back into his house.

"Nigga, don't even try me! See dat dot on ya head, don't make me put ah bullet in it!" Mar Mar's connect tried to reach for his strap, but was stopped by Tae.

"Yo! Get dat nigga's strap." Tae told CNN. And get dat bitch ass niggas strap, too. I know he got one on him."

"Give it up, nigga." CNN said disarming Mar Mar. "Aight, give me yours too, bitch ass nigga!" CNN said to the connect.

"Now march ya'll asses in the house. It's time to play find da dope and money, ma'fuckas." Tae told Mar Mar and his connect. But he was surprised to see Money in her bra, panties, and silk robe, holding an AK 47.

"DROP Y'ALL MUTHAFUCKIN' GUNS!" Money yelled out shaking as she aimed her assault rifle at Tae and CNN.

"Bitch, is you crazy! I'll blow ya nigga's brains all over ya pretty li'l face," said CNN.

"Now put da choppa down!" Tae hollered.

"Yo! You betta put that fuckin' choppa down, bitch!" CNN didn't know what was going on. Seeing Money pointing an AK 47 at them confused him and made him nervous.

"Babe, just put it down. I'ma just give these niggas what they want. What they came fo'." Mar Mar said shrugging his shoulders and shaking his head.

"See, dat's what I'm talkin' 'bout," said Tae.

"Now give me dat choppa," CNN said slowly walking over to Money with piercing eyes.

"Just give it to him," Mar Mar told Money.

CNN took the choppa off of Money and struck her with it, then motioned like he was going to hit her again.

"Oof!" Money toppled backwards.

"No, man. NO!" Mar Mar cried out. *"Stop! I'll give you everything, just don't kill us!"*

After the safe was cleaned out, the connect, Mar Mar, and Money laid on the floor with their hands zip-tied behind their backs.

Tae made sure Money's zip-ties were loose enough for her to free her hands.

"Ugh…Ugh…I…I think I can get loose." Money said to Mar Mar wiggling her hands out of the white, plastic band wrapped around her wrist.

The connect wiggled and squirmed trying to free himself never taking his eyes of off the AK 47 the robbers left behind.

"There, I'm out," Money said finally freeing herself. She stood up, rubbing her wrist.

"Cut me loose, babe." Mar Mar told Money.

Money looked around the bedroom for something to cut the zip-ties with. Taking a pair of scissors, she cut the connect loose first because he was the closest to her. Then she cut Mar Mar loose.

"Who was that?" The connect asked.

"I don't…Hol' up…What da…" Mar Mar attempted to answer the connect's question, but was at a loss for words when he turned around, and saw the connect pointing the AK 47 at him and Money. Money ran out the room.

"DOOMP! DOOMP! DOOMP! DOOMP!" A volley of bullets followed her out of the bedroom, tearing holes through the bedroom walls.

Mar Mar was frozen in his tracks. The connect turned the assault rifle back on Mar Mar. "I think you set me the fuck up!" He said to Mar Mar with a menacing look on his face,

"Is you crazy? Why would I rob myself?"

"You know I had more than just ya work in the van, or maybe you thought that I would give you a pass cause we both got robbed. But I know they gon' give you ya shit back. "

"Naaaw, dawg. You know me. You know I'm not gon' try you like dat."

"One of y'all did this shit. Either way somebody slipped and it wasn't me. So y'all gotta pay fo' this. I got people I gotta answer to so y'all gotta answer fo' this shit." The connect lifted the AK and aimed it at Mar Mar.

149

"COME ON, BRUH...YOU KNOW..." Were his last words.

"DOOMP! DOOMP! DOOMP! DOOMP! DOOMP!" The connect let off a barrage of shots hitting Mar Mar in the upper body, splitting his chest wide open, and tearing a chunk out of his skull, blowing it all over the bedroom.

Hearing the gunshots, Money ran into the woods with her cell phone in hand.

Looking around the bedroom, the connect searched for Mar Mar's car keys. Patting Mar Mar's pockets, he felt what he believed to be them. "Got 'em." He knew that the gunshots were heard, and the police were on their way so he tried to hurry. He never even thought about Money getting away. Once he got away he knew they would never see each other again.

Picking up the AK, he ran outside. Just as he thought his van was gone, along with his cell phone and twenty kilos of cocaine.

Out of breath, Money called Tae. "Money?" He answered.

"Ah…Ah, come get me. I'm scared, Tae. He's try'na kill me," Money frantically told Tae. Gazing from the darkness of the wooded area, she saw the connect getting into Mar Mar's Bentley, but as he was pulling off, the police were pulling up. The police car lights lit up the house.

"TURN THE CAR OFF!" A police officer yelled over a speaker.

"What da…Where are you?" Tae asked Money. He heard the police yelling in the background of their conversation.

"I'm in the woods…Hm…Ah, the police got the connect pulled over.

"DOOMP! DOOMP! DOOMP! DOOMP! DOOMP! DOOMP!" The connect fired into the police car, fatally wounding its driver.

"POP! POP! POP!" The police on the passenger side of the cruiser exited the car and fired three rounds into the connect, killing him instantly. Sheltered on the side of the car he radioed in. "OFFICER DOWN!"

"Oooh, no, they killed him!" Money broke down, witnessing the murder of the connect.

"MONEY?! MONEY?!" Tae yelled into the phone. "TURN AROUND, YO!" Tae told CNN. "MONEY, WHO GOT KILLED?!" He asked Money.

"The cops killed him."

"The cops killed who, Money?" Tae asked again.

"The connect! They killed the connect!"

"We turning around. We on the way to get you. Go through the woods until you see the street at the bottom of his spot. Don't come out of the woods till you see us. We in ah van. We'll be there in ah few minutes."

Smack Down, exited the shower at an Edgewood Estate he went to almost every night. It was one of the places he went to escape the street life. Stuck, staring at himself in the steamy bathroom mirror, he ran his fingers over the two bullet wounds in his chest. Thinking about the gunfire that nearly took his life. There was a scar that ran down the center of his chest from the operation that saved his life. The near death experience came courtesy of Mr. Frosty Blow's strap.

After stumbling upon his sister's large stash of money, Mr. Frosty Blow forced a confession out of her. Which explained Tae's new found success, and his sister being questioned by homicide detectives. He was told her boyfriend had died during a home invasion. He didn't know that Tae was behind it, and had used his sister to set it up.

Once they graduated from high school, Money stayed confined to her bedroom, not wanting to be bothered by no one, not even Tae. Mr. Frosty Blow just taught that it was because she had lost her boyfriend, but he had finally gotten the truth out of her. And he knew why she was acting so strange.

Hearing every detail about the jack, except for CNN's name, Mr. Frosty Blow replayed everything that had taken place after her boyfriend's death, in his head. Tae had claimed he found a new connect, and had served him several kilos for a cheaper price then he was getting them for. He had bought matching Bentleys for his sister, Money, and himself, moved into a baby mansion, and bought a state-of- the-art studio. He had even changed his name to "Smack Down," and started rapping. Inspired by his favorite rapper, Project Pat.

Rushing to Smack Down's studio after it all had set in, he rushed inside, pulled his strap and shot Tae twice. "Stay the fuck away from my sister," was all Tae recalled after waking up from his operation surrounded by family and friends, including a teary-eyed Money. Then Money had Tae's baby, and shortly after that tragedy struck.

Smack Down, stared at the image of himself in the foggy mirror and shook his head. Thinking about how far he had come. And if no one understood, he understood that every action causes a reaction. That was one of the reasons why he was being cautious when it came to dealing with Mr. Frosty Blow. That along with something deep inside of him that allowed him to still love the man that had tried to kill him.

Now some young, dumb ass wannabe was trying to force his hand. Trying to convince him that his son's uncle should be eliminated. Smack Down shook his head again, and walked away from the mirror.

"Dad?" Octavius, Smack Down and Money's son, called out. "Mom wants you." Octavius told his father.

Going into the bedroom, Tae glanced at Money as she sat up on the bed. She looked prettier than ever. This day was her birthday, and she had plans of enjoying it with   close friends and family.

"You ready?" Tae asked.

"Yes, I'm ready to start my day." Money said, with a big smile on her face.

Placing his arms under Money's body, he hoisted her up. Money wrapped her arms around his neck as Tae sat her in her automatic wheelchair. After Money had their son, she had been shot by Mar Mar's brother. She survived the shooting, but had lost the use of her legs.

Seeing Money this way hurt Tae, but he was happy that she survived as he did for the sake of their son.

YOU WIN SOME/YOU LOSE SOME

At Monte Bucks Enterprises, the cast of LTMP sat at the boardroom table. GQ Dawg, Smack Down, Boom Bap, and America on one side. Dominican Flames, Mr. Frosty Blow, Blocks N Bricks, and Making Hitz on the other.

Monte Bucks at the head of one side of the table, and the opposite side of him was prepared for the other Executive Producer, but she sat out of this meeting due to other more important business.

Monte Bucks had got word about America and Dominican Flames' beef, and also knew that it had escalated to Dominican Flames' Sprinter van being shot up. Hearing this, Monte Bucks had his lawyer draw up a disclaimer that stated that the company would not be responsible for any illegal actions of its cast members, and he wanted them all to sign it or exit the show. He also wanted to inform them of Hip Hop Weekly doing a LTMP Edition of their Magazine.

"Today, I'm flying in Hip Hop Weekly. Matter of fact, they should have landed already. Anyway, everybody will have a chance to give an interview. GQ Dawg is doing a video shoot tomorrow. It's gonna last all day and end at Reflections…"

"Why eh' thang gotta be at Reflections?" America muttered sucking her teeth.

"Fuck you bitch! You ain't gotta come!" Dominican Flames shot back.

"Whoa! Whoa! Hol' up! It's gon' be at Reflections because I'm keeping everything in house. Why would I give another club the exposure?" Monte Bucks explained.

"That bitch shot my shit up! She lucky she able to go anywhere!" Dominican Flames stood up and said.

"Bitch, I don't know what the fuck you talking about!" America stood up as well and said.

"I bet you don't! Just like you don't know about my footage. Lying ass bitch!" Dominican Flames said. Her blood was boiling.

"SIT DOWN! Sit y'all asses down!"

American and Dominican Flames sat down. The boardroom was the only place security was not needed when it came to the cast members. Even though they stood close by, on the outside of the Boardroom door. Hearing all of the commotion, they rushed in, but Monte Bucks waved them off. He didn't need security to control his employee. All he needed to do was raise his voice, and show that he meant business.

"Like I was saying," Monte Bucks continued his speech. "Dawg is doin' his video tomorrow, and I would like to congratulate him and Making Hitz…"

Boom Bap and Making Hitz's eyes connected.

"Fo' their hit single *She Like It from Da Back*, being number four on the Billboard charts, and number one on USA Today's Urban Airplay charts."

Everybody applauded.

"And GQ is featured in the *Song of the Week* section of *USA Today*. And, I don't know if any of y'all have been paying any attention, but I wanna proudly say that our Teaser has close to forty million views. So everybody keep up the good work. We'll meet up next week, regular time. Oh, and if y'all haven't, make sure y'all give our other Executive Producer, Money, ah birthday shout out." Monte Bucks concluded, and everyone started to exit the Boardroom having small conversations with each other.

"Monte, let me holler at you fo' ah sec'," Mr. Frosty Blow said approaching Monte Bucks.

During the meeting, America had caught Smack Down staring at her several times. Leaving the meeting he stopped her in her tracks.

"What was you doin' wit' that sucka ass nigga, Frosty, the other night?" He

Asked.

"He ain't no sucka, and we did ah song, Smack Down!" America replied with a coy smile on her face.

"You comin' to Money's birthday dinner?" Smack Down asked.

"Doubt it. That's my mom's girl. We sent her ah birthday video this morning. But I wouldn't feel right being there without my mother. I really don't know her like that. Hold up, that's ya baby moms, right?"

"Yea yup, but hey I wanna do ah song wit' you too, though." Smack Down changed the subject. "Take my number down." Smack Down said.

"Aight." America pulled out her phone.

Smack down took it, and put his number in. "Let's set somethin' up wit the show."

"SMACK! Yo! Let me yell atcha, dukes." Making Hitz interrupted their gathering.

"Hey, I'll holler at you later. I'm on my way to see my moms." America said, before she walked off.

"Cool. Hit me later, though," Smack Down said.

"Aight," America said walking towards the elevator.

"HOLLA AT ME!" Smack Down playfully yelled.

"I SAID AIGHT!" America turned her head and yelled back with a chuckle.

Inside the elevator, America watched as the elevator numbers counted down to the garage level. TING! The elevator door slid open. The sound of America's Giuseppe spiked suede wedge sandals bounced off the concrete echoed throughout the garage. Reaching in her YSL Cassandre leather clutch for her Lambo' Aventador keys, she was caught by surprise by two men running up on her. Her life flashed before her eyes. "OH GOD!"

PIP! PIP! PIP! PIP! PIP!

"Aaaah…Oh my god…Oh my god!" America yelped.

The shots from the two paint ball guns the shooters yielded, covered her Maje printed silk jersey, and made her drop her clutch. Her iPhone, covered in its Maschino hard case, dropped and bounced off of the ground.

Then a lyrical copper Rolls-Royce Wraith pulled up, slowly, and Dominican Flames stepped out of it.

"Next time, bitch, it won't be paint. You'll be covered in blood," she said then got back into her Wraith with her two henchmen and pulled off.

"BITCH! YOU BITCH! IT'S ON!" America screamed watching them pull off.

"Hey miss, you okay?" A stranger walked up to America and asked. "I seen the whole thing. I was watchin' from my car," he said.

"Yea, I… UGH! Suddenly as America was talking, the stranger struck her twice with the

butt of his gun, knocking her out.

At Money's birthday dinner, a small group of family and friends gathered at a private location, to

163

celebrate Money's born date, including Monte Bucks. The cast members of LTMP, sent gifts and birthday wishes.

Money wasn't too fond of being around strangers. Plus, she was over protective of her son, and didn't allow strangers to even see what he looked like. After being shot she was extra careful about who she associated with.

"TINK! TINK! TINK! TINK! TINK! Um-um," Mr. Frosty Blow tapped his fork against his Ace of Spade's bottle to get everybody's attention. "Um-Um," he cleared his throat again. "Sis, on behalf of everyone here…" Mr. Frosty Blow paused and looked at Smack Down who sat beside his sister, Money, and their son. "And everybody that's a part of the show, we wanna thank you. If it wasn't for your vision, and Monte Bucks'…"

Everybody laughed. Monte Bucks raised his glass.

"No seriously, if it wasn't for y'all we wouldn't be here. Close to forty million views? That's big. I just wanna thank y'all. I wanna thank you sis."

Everybody applauded.

Smack Down's phone vibrated for the third time since Mr. Frosty Blow started his speech. Hitter B had called him several times before this, but this time it was CNN, so he had to take the call.

As everyone saluted Money by raising their glasses or tapping the

silverware against their champagne flutes, Smack Down leaned towards Money to whisper in her ear.

"I need to take this call, looks important." He told Money.

"Okay." Money understood.

"And I know shit's gon' get bigga and bigga." Mr. Frosty Blow said taking his seat. "Yo! where da fuck you goin'?" He asked Smack Down feeling disrespected by Smack Down leaving the table while he was still speaking.

"Bro, don't do that, please...Not here, not now." Money said to her brother.

Smack Down walked away as if he never heard a word Mr. Frosty Blow was saying. Everybody at the table

165

knew about their story, but knew that they both had enough respect for Money to not start anything around her. She wasn't having it.

"YO! WHAT'S SO FUCKIN' IMPORTANT THAT YOU MA'FUCKAS KEEP CALLIN' ME? Y'ALL KNOW I'M AT DINNER WIT' MONEY AND MY SON!" Smack Down said into the phone, holding it with a death grip to his mouth. The disturbance had him hot. "WHAT?! You bullshittin'! Where he got her? You there now, you wit him? Be right over!" Now Smack Down understood why CNN was calling him. Hitter B had kidnapped America and he was beating her to a bloody pulp for information on the whereabouts of her money. Not only was Hitter B threatening to take away his son's mother's brother, he was doing shit that could get them all locked up for life. Smack Down knew how to keep the streets separated from his family, but now Hitter B was bringing the streets to his family.

"Money, I gotta go, some'in' crazy just happened." Smack Down whispered in Money's ear.

"Some street shit?" Money asked, looking at Smack Down with her nostrils flared, and an angry look on her face.

"Sort of," Smack Down answered.

"See, that's why we ain't together. You just can't leave the streets alone. Just go! I don't care, bye!"

Smack Down rubbed the top of his son's head. "Dad gotta step out. I'll see you later. Love you," Smack Down said kissing his son on the forehead.

"Hey, I wanna thank eh'body fo' comin' out to celebrate Money's b-day. But sorry I gotta slip out on some business," Smack Down told the dinner guests. Money smacked her teeth, and rolled her eyes. "Mm mm mm."

"What da fuck you mean you gotta go on some business shit? We all got business to handle. Family comes first though, yo!" Mr. Frosty said standing up at the table. "First, you disrespect me, then you gon' disrespect my sista," he expressed.

"Man, I gotta go! I ain't try'na hear that shit you talkin'," Smack

Down said on his way out of the restaurant.

"What da fuck you say, nigga?" Mr. Frosty Blow wanted to go after Smack Down, but Money put her hand up and hushed him.

"Bro, let him go, please."

***

Smack Down arrived at the Bass-Filled Recording Studio.

"He got her upstairs in the recording room one. Oh boy beat the shit outta her. He got plastic down under her and eh'thing." CNN told Smack Down as he let him into the studio.

"What da fuck, man! Why da fuck you ain't stop him?" Smack Down asked CNN with a look of disappointment on his face.

"I did! That nigga did most of that shit before I got here. He got that girl's face fucked up. She told him that she had a millticket somewhere. He said he wasn't gon' make ah move till you got here. And he said Dominican Flames and her goons hit her up wit' paint ball guns before he grabbed her up. So most of the red shit she's covered in is paint." CNN told Smack Down.

"What da fuck kinda shit is that?" Smack Down asked.

"He said Dominican Flames told America next time it was gon' be blood an' shit." CNN told Smack Down what Hitter B said he heard before he kidnapped America.

"Now that bitch is ah killa. This reality TV shit got ma'fuckas goin' crazy." Smack Down was referring to Dominican Flames.

Hitter B had taken America to their newly renovated studio where her cries would go unheard. Smack Down had given Hitter B a hundred thousand dollars to upgrade his studio. Instead Hitter B had bought an old car lot and turned the duplex complex into a state of the art studio with all of the up to date equipment and renovated it. The upper level was sound proofed and remodeled.

Hitter B was a mild mannered young boy from the hood, but sometime during the first season of LTMP he had got turned on to Percocet and Molly, and started doing things that he thought would make him fit in. Smack Down normally ignored his hard acting persona, but now Hitter B had taken things to another level, kidnapping and torture.

"Aaaah ...Helllp!" America screamed.

"SCREAM ALL YOU WANT, BITCH! Can't nobody hear ya dumb ass! Dis muthafucka's soundproof! So scream all you want!"

"Helllp!"

Smack Down and CNN heard America scream when they opened the door to the recording room, but didn't hear anything before that. America and Hitter B's screams and yells were absorbed by the cellulose fiber panels and special acoustical polyurethane foam tiles that covered the walls.

Hitter B slapped America hard across her face.

"Why are you doin' this?! I told you, you can have the money! Please, please don't kill me!" America pleaded.

Hitter B. popped America with his pistol. "Shut up, hoe!" He ordered. "Bitch, gotta mill- ticket!" Hitter B told Smack Down with a devilish grin on his face. Smack Down could tell that he was high off of something.

"Let me holla at you, fam'." Smack Down said to Hitter B waving him over to him.

"Smack please." America continued to plead.

"I TOLD YA ASS TO SHUT UP, BITCH!" Hitter B said pointing his strap at America.

CNN shook his head watching Hitter B.

"What nigga? You gotta problem?" Hitter B asked CNN.

"Let me holla at you, yo!" Smack Down said again in a firmer voice.

171

Hitter B went over to Smack Down. "What up, big bro? We on, my nigga. All we gotta do is make ah call and collect da paper." Hitter B told Smack Down.

"Yea, that's what's up. Let me ask you ah question. Did you tell anybody 'bout this…You know…This, this ideal of yours?" Smack Down asked.

"Nah bruh. I was gon' let you know but I knew you was gon' be busy today. And I knew y'all had that meeting today so shit was perfect fo' me to grab her, you know?"

"I feel you. You got plastic down, the whole shit."

"Well, you know, bro, I ain't try'na leave her blood in ya spot."

"Right, so get the number off her so we can collect." Smack Down muttered.

"You know we gotta kill this bitch," Hitter B told Smack Down.

"Kill her?" Smack Down questioned.

"Hell yea. She knows who did this to her. We can't take no chances. The good thing about it is eh'body'll think that bitch Dominican Flames did the shit, you know?" Hitter B had everything worked out.

"Yea, you right. We can't let her testify on us." Smack Down agreed with Hitter B. "Aight, let's do this. Yo, you came up on this, bro." Smack Down said to Hitter B, slapping his hand five, pulling him close, and hugging him.

Hitter B hugged Smack Down tightly, released him, and smiled at him.

"We came up, big bro," Hitter B told Smack Down. Then he turned towards America to get more information. "Bitch, where was…"

Smack Down blew a hole in the back of Hitter B's head, walked up to him after he fell, and shot him in the head again, making sure he was dead.

"AAAAH! NOOO!" America screamed.

"Stupid ma'fucka," Smack Down said tucking his strap back into his waist. "Untie her," he told CNN.

America sobbed. Her heart was beating frantically at a fast rapid pace.

"You gon' be aight," CNN told America as he untied her. "'Bout time you killed that nigga," he said to Smack Down. "What we gon' do wit' her?" He asked.

"I'm takin' her home," Smack Down said.

"Aaaw, thank you," America ran to Smack Down and hugged him.

"And him?" CNN asked looking over at the remains of Hitter B's skull.

"Let one of da li'l homies find him. They got keys. They'll find his ass. And get rid of the rope, chair, and ya clothes." Smack Down told CNN.

"What about his car?" CNN asked. "Leave it." Smack Down answered.

I'M MY SISTA'S KEEPER

In the wee early hours of the kidnapping, Smack Down drove America to her Fox Chapel estate.

"Thank you, Smack," America said holding a rag to one of the gashes on her face. Looking at her wounds in the visor mirror. At first, she was skeptical about Smack Down knowing where she lived, but the more she thought about him putting two bullets into her captor, the more trusting of him she became. Besides that, she had called her brother, and told him that she had been hurt, and Smack Down was bringing her home. She knew that would raise a red flag with her brother, and he would be on point about anything that would take place when they arrived.

"Look, America, I'm truly sorry about what happened." Smack Down murmured shaking his head. "I didn't know anything about that nigga's plans of kidnapping you," he told her.

"Shit, I'm just glad you were there to save me. He was going to kill me, wasn't he?"

"Hmph." Smack Down briefly closed his eyes and shook the thought of Hitter B killing America out of his head. "Yea, yup, that was his plan." He confirmed Hitter B's murderous ways of thinking.

"I owe you my life, Smack." America said releasing a thankful sigh.

"Nah, you don't owe me shit. Matter of fact, send me ya medical bill. I got that."

"Ha, you want me to bill you $6.00?"

"What you mean $6.00," Smack Down looked over at America nursing her injuries.

"Make this right, Smack. I'm saying I'm not going to the hospital. I'm just gon' pop a couple Advils and call it ah night. I just want to take a hot bath and crawl into my bed," America said as she directed Smack Down to her luxury estate.

"Man, you crazy. You going to the hospital even if I gotta take you. You might have ah concussion or some'in'." Smack Down cautioned her.

"They're going to ask too many questions. What am I going to tell them? I got beat by a crazed kidnapper named Hitter B? I can't do that, now can I? And if I did that they'll link the dead body lying in your studio to me." America improvised.

"Damn, I ain't think about that," Smack down said scratching his head, checking for loose ends he may have mentally left untied.

"I'll be aight. I'ma big girl. A couple ice packs, a couple Advils and my bed, and I'll be just fine. But like I said, I owe you," America said looking over at Smack Down with a half-smile on her face. Smack Down smiled back at her. "If you need anything let me know," America said.

"Aight, maybe there is some'in' you can do fo' me…" Smack Down paused and stroked his goatee with his hand. "Invest some of that paper into my next move. I'm try'na make ah couple mo' moves, and get out of the game. If you invest, we can make dat happen."

"Oh, you try'na cop big, and quit the game, huh? Make this left." America asked as she continued to direct Smack Down to her estate.

"What you know about coppin'?" Smack Down asked.

"My grandma and my mom taught me eh' thang there is to know 'bout the streets. My grandma was one of da biggest drug dealers in our 'hood in the 80's and the 90's. That's how we know that bitch Dominican. My grandma did time fo' coppin' big off of her father. When she got outta jail she fell back and got into real estate. She the one that got this spot fo' my moms, and a few other spots fo' people on the show. So, you know, I know about the game." America explained. "Go up this driveway." She continued.

"Daaaamn, this ya spot?" Smack Down looked at the estate in awe. "This joint is insane," he said.

"Thank you." America said getting her belongings together to exit the car.

"So you gon' make this power move wit' me?" Smack Down asked pulling into the driveway of America's 6.2-acre estate.

"Whateva you need just let me know. I got you." America said.

"Five hundred racks. I'm try'na go hard."

"I got you."

"Yo A', what da fuck happened!" America's brother asked running up to Smack Down's Phantom trying to pry the door open to get to his sister.

Smack Down unlocked the door for him.

"I'ma fuckin' kill some-fuckin'-body...Who da fuck!" Ren walked side to side. "Who da fuck did this shit, sis'?"

"Bro calm down! I took care of it." America told her brother as she stepped out of Smack Down's luxury car.

"Bro, I'm cool." She told him trying to back him up from herself. "Hey Smack, holla at me in the mornin', early." She told Smack Down.

"Bet. What's early, though?" He asked/

"'Bout six. If it's not, then we gon' have to wait till tomorrow night. I'm pickin' my mom up from the hospital at nine."

"Oh yea? That's what's up."

"A', come on! Hooker's on his way over. We gon' do some'in' 'bout this shit!"   Ren was getting impatient.

"I'll be here at six."

"Cool see you then," America said blowing him a kiss."

"Don't play," he told her smiling before he pulled off.

"LISTEN! Either you and the two sucka ass nigga that hit my sista up with them paint balls meet me or shit gon' really go down. You know I don't give ah fuck 'bout

no TV show or none of that shit! Y'all ma'fuckas ain't gon'
keep disrespectin' my family, my sista…Well, meet me. I
just wanna holla at them niggas. We can put the guns
down, unless that's what you want. Yea, no guns. You got
my word …Wherever. Langley High School parking lot. I'll
be there in ah half." After America told her brother what
happened he called Dominican Flames. He couldn't get
revenge on the dead man lying in Smack Down's studio,
but he definitely planned on settling the score with
Dominican Flames and her street goons. He wanted to kill
them, but America begged him not to bring any more heat
to their family. She explained how it would be bad
business, and would possibly lead to an investigation that
neither of their families needed.

***

The clock on Ren's cell phone was approaching
1:00 A.M. The night was still young for those that played
in the streets. He mentally prepared himself for hand-to-
hand combat as his tires hissed, rolling over the terrain into
Langley High School's parking lot. Head lights shined and
lit up the faces of Ren and his two passengers as they
pulled in, parked, and got out of the car.

"You might need my help, bro," Hooker said.

"Mines too," America agreed. "Them some big ma'fuckas," she said with a chuckle.

"I got this," Ren said stepping out of the car into the ring of headlights, TV show divas, and street fighters.

The fist of a humungous enforcer slamming into his hand sounded like a baseball slamming into a mit.

Ren, removed his hoodie but left his wife-beater on. His muscular body was heavily tattooed with Japanese and Asian artwork; skulls, dragons, tigers and Samurai masks. He stood 5'9, 250 pounds of well sculpted flesh tailor fitted to every muscle in his body. He cracked his knuckles and neck, sizing his opponents up.

His opponents were also muscle heads, standing imminently around their lady boss, Dominican Flames. The four giants stood over her like mountains. They all oozed of toughness, and all were known to live in the violent world as bodyguards, hard asses and street thugs with a reputation for murder.

Dominican Flames' doormen and bodyguards knew nothing of Ren, as he knew nothing of them. They knew nothing of each other's training or fighting experiences. On the other hand, Dominican Flames knew almost everything about Ren. They had grown up together and even had an interest in one another up until his grandmother was indicted for her father's mistakes. Ren blamed her father for his grandmother's arrest and indictment.

Since then there had always been some animosity between them. A smoldering enmity, their mother and grandmother overlooked. They understood the actions and consequences of the game.

Their grandmother's success was owed to Dominican Flames' parents.

What America and Ren didn't know was their grandmother was gratefully rewarded for her loyalty. But at this point none of that mattered. Ren was ready to punish, even kill, those that had threatened his sister.

Before they had arrived, Dominican Flames, started to tell her men for hire about Ren's four-year military background. She knew that he had taken up martial arts when they were kids, and about his one punch knock out, but she didn't want to scare her guys. Besides they were also skillful fighters. Men on both sides knew the one wrong move, no matter how skillful you were, could send the most trained fighter into a panic, making them forget all about what they were taught to do.

During his military years, Ren traveled and learned about different cultures and styles of hand combat, including Judo and kickboxing. He veered these fighting styles towards, more practical, full-contact, street style martial arts. His teacher had once graced the cover of Black Belt Magazine. Now his skills stood to be challenged by hired, fully trained, licensed security guards.

When the security guard saw Ren take off his hoodie, he removed his suit jacket and tie and handed them to another bodyguard.

"I'ma tear ya ass apart, boy!" He said to Ren in Spanish.

"I don't know what the fuck he just said, but it sounded scary." Hooker joked not afraid at all. He had also gone to the military training with Ren, and knew a few fighting techniques himself. He was also deadly with his hands. If he wanted to he could crush another man with his bare hands. He had killed shortly before this grudge match and was not afraid to do it again.

America and Dominican Flames gazed at each other. Their nostrils flared as did their tempers.

Ren and the bodyguard squared up to fight. There would be no mercy given, and neither of them were seeking forgiveness. Moving in a 180-degree direction, the bodyguard moved light on his feet. Ren took notice of his possible training in martial arts. Standing off from the guard, Ren's eyes locked into his opponent's movements. He wanted him to move in, but wouldn't allow him to move in too close. He knew that could be fatal. But yet, he needed him to come in close enough for his short reach.

After a few seconds, Ren realized the bodyguard was waiting on the same thing. So Ren gave him what he was waiting for. Moving in on the guard, Ren's shorter body bobbed with buoyancy.

Similar to Iron Mike Tyson, he bobbed and weaved and threw a machine gun-like volley of punches. One caught the bodyguard once on the left side of his face, leaving his ear ringing. Seeing Ren retreating, made the bodyguard move in. "Aaaarrggh," he came at Ren like a bear, arms and claws extended for the kill. Ren waited for the guard to get within arms-length and stepped to the side sending the guard flying passed him. The scene was like that of a bull charging a matador. As the bodyguard flew passed him, Ren threw a right hand punch that struck the guard in the left temple. The impact of the blow sent the large man plummeting, perpendicular to the ground face first. He was unconscious before he hit the hard concrete. The hit of force split the guard's head wide open. Flesh and blood smeared on the harsh texture of the gravel, tearing his skin into shreds of brown meat and white flesh as blood trailed.

Ren, looked back over his shoulder at the large structure of man that collapsed like a falling sky scraper. Then he pointed to the bodyguard holding the other guard's coat.

"You! Come on, let's go!"

After a few seconds, Ren realized the bodyguard
was waiting on the same thing. So Ren gave him what he
was waiting for. Moving in on the guard, Ren's shorter
body bobbed with buoyancy.

While they continued to fight, a third bodyguard
grabbed the first bodyguard under his arms, and dragged
the dead sack of flimsy bone and muscle off to the side.

Dominican Flames shook her head. "This is
pathetic! Look at these muthafuckas." She said
disappointed in her security.

Hooker watched the third bodyguard to make sure
he wasn't trying to do anything to help his friends. Deep
inside he wished he would so he could join in on the action.
He was proud of how Ren was handling himself, but he
was tired of watching. It was getting boring.

Seeing the third guard moving in his peripheral,
Ren lost focus for a minute which was just enough time for
the bodyguard to swing a punch. Ren saw it too late and
was struck in the face. His nose immediately began to
bleed.

Hooker started walking towards the third bodyguard.

"YO! Back the fuck off, Hooker! I got this," Ren told his man wiping blood from his face with the back of his hand.

"Maaan pssss, whatever," Hooker let out a frustrated sigh.

America watched, still feeling the pain from the whooping she had took earlier. Her stomach churned, she was shaking from an adrenaline rush. She just wanted to go home and go to sleep. She had seen and been through enough for one day.

Dominican Flames looked over at America, examining her swollen face and black eye. She tried to figure out where the fresh injuries came from. She knew that her men didn't cause them. "Oh my god, this bitch done beat herself up for attention. Now Ren think we did that shit. Stinkin' ass bitch!" She thought.

"I'ma end this right now!" The second bodyguard sneered in Spanish.

"Yea, end this shit!" Dominican Flames said.

"What the fuck did he say?" Hooker asked America.

"Something about ending it." America answered. She understood Spanish a little bit. Her mother and grandmother spoke Spanish fluently. Ren did also. She never cared for the language enough to learn it.

A small amount of time had elapsed, but Ren felt he had been there too long. He also wanted to end the hand to hand combat, but he refused to submit or rush himself into a mistake. Ren threw his own series of kicks. He kicked at the guard's head twice. The second guard blocked both kicks. But what happened next caught the second guard by surprise. Ren dropped low and took the second guard off of his feet with a leg sweep. The second guard landed on his back, and as he tried to recover, Ren kicked him in the face multiple times. The guard covered himself. Then he grabbed Ren by the foot and twisted it sending Ren to the ground off balance.

Gathering themselves, both men were back on their feet bobbing back and forth again searching for each other's weakness. Then Ren stopped dancing, and so did the second bodyguard. He felt that Ren had had enough and walked up to him. "UGH!" Ren head butted him and followed that with a punch to the throat crushing his voice box in his 22-inch neck.

"WHOOF!" The second bodyguard gasped. Then Ren made his fingers stiff in a scissor formation into each of his eyes.

"MM! You muthafucka! "Ren sputtered.

"Oooh fuck…Uh…Uh! "The second guard goggled out. Stepping back away from Ren, he tried to shake the stars from his eyes. Plus, escape any further punishment.

Ren stepped into the second bodyguard's imaginary and kicked hard. He snapped the second bodyguard's kneecap inward. "Ooooh, shit!" The second bodyguard wailed a wheezy gasp as he collapsed.

Breathing heavily, Ren then walked over to Dominican Flames. Her bodyguards stood in front of her to protect her. Even the one that had got beat up first. She

I Need A Bawss In My Life

moved them to the side and walked up to Ren. He didn't scare her. He had actually turned her on.

"The next time you come for us, me, my sista, you better kill us, or you won't live to see another day. Neither of you!" Ren said.

Dominican Flames pecked Ren on his lips. Ren wiped her kiss away. "You got my pussy so wet, you should come home with me, Turn ah fighter into ah lover, baby." Dominican Flames told Ren making his dick hard.

"Get the fuck outta here! Like I said, you better come correct next time."

"I'm good. I got what I wanted, baby. Well, I wish I had a man like you in my life," Dominican Flames said to Ren.

"Whatever," Ren said walking away.

"What the fuck she mean she got what she wanted?" America asked her brother.

191

"Who knows what that crazy bitch is talking about," Ren said. "Maybe she wanted her guards to get their asses kicked for being dumb enough to fuck with you."

They all laughed as Ren drove off.

"Get him up! Get him up, now! Y'all some sorry ass ma'fuckas. Y'all lucky y'all ass whoopin' is coming with ah price, or I would have all y'all killed." She told her security. Inside of her SUV, she scrolled down her phone to Monte Bucks' number and pressed send. After a couple rings he answered.

"Hello, Monte Bucks."

"Monte, this is Dominican. I got some exclusive footage fo' you that's sure to boost the ratings. Not even TMZ can get their hands on this," Dominican Flames said looking at the dash-cam, mounted in her truck.

MONEY & MURDA

In the movies when a dealer made a massive drug deal it would take place at some kind of warehouse surrounded by shady Uzi-totting goons, lurking in every shadow. But with Smack Down that wasn't the case. After doing business with each other for close to a decade, him and his connect had built a bond and fully trusted each other. So neither of them needed back up. They both believed that the less people involved, the better. But knowing something could go wrong at any given time, they still took precautions.

Over the years they developed a set step-by-step process of doing things. And while using this strategy they had never been jacked or investigated as far as they knew. Smack Down would send the money. His connect's most trusted middleman would drop the work off at a motel used by semi-truck drivers, CNN would pick up the work, and cut and stash it until it was ready to be delivered. Smack Down sent the money, the middleman delivered the work,

193

CNN picked up, processed and re-delivered that work, and Smack Don and the connect oversaw the operation.

Driving to America's estate, Smack Down thought about the time he jacked Mar Mar and his connect at a place similar to hers. In almost ten years nothing had changed; everything ran smooth. All the same players were in place, but this time there would be an addition to the team. If America came through with the five-hundred thousand she would become an equal partner, and they would be copping more work than he ever did. But he would not allow her to come in and disrupt his effective way of doing things. No money was worth that.

These were some of the things going through Smack Down's mind as he pulled into her driveway. He had called America at 5:30 A.M. and was surprised when she answered his call on the first ring. She had told him that she had been up since five waiting for his call. Grabbing his phone off of the passenger seat, he scrolled down to America's number and pressed send. "I'm here," Smack Down told America. Less than a minute later she came to the door and waved him in.

"New car, huh?" America asked Smack Down, holding the door open for him as he walked in.

Smack Down looked back at his 2001 Windstar. It was the van he did his dirt in. "Yea, I'm try'na impress you," he told her.

"You already did. Come up to my room," she said with a smile on her face.

"How you feelin'?" Smack Down asked watching America's ass sway back and forth in her thin Mickey Mouse printed pajama pants as he followed her up the steps.

Inside of her room, Ren finished rubber banding the five-hundred thousand sprawled across the bed. "What up," he said to Smack Down.

"Sup, fam!" Smack Down asked.

"Let's put the money in this bag." America took an overnight bag out of her closet and put it on the bed.

Smack Down helped her throw stacks of money in the bag. "How much is this," he asked.

"Five-hunid stacks. Ain't that what you asked fo'. How much I'ma make, though?" America was uncertain of what to expect back. She wanted to make it clear.

Ren looked up waiting for Smack Down's answer as he helped them throw more of the money into the bag.

"First of all, of course I'm gonna match you. So we goin' in wit' ah mill' ticket. Now let me show you," Smack Down pulled out his cell phone, and pulled up the calculator. "At twenty racks ah brick, we'll get fifty bricks for ah mill. I'll turn that into seventy-five of them thangs, and…" Smack Down punched 75x\$32,000 into the calculator and pressed the equal sign. \$2,400,000 popped up on the LCD screen.

"2.4 mill', that's what I'm talking about! You hear that, bro?!" America asked Ren.

Ren put his head down as he threw the last of the stacks into the overnight bag acting like he wasn't paying attention to what they were talkin' 'bout or doing. "Nah, what's that sis'?" He asked, but Smack Down peeped his game. It was something that Smack Down wasn't feeling about him, and that shady move really made him feel uncomfortable around Ren. He didn't like fake ass niggas.

"He said we gon' make 2.4 million off this deal right here."

"That's what's up," he said zipping the bag up and handing it to Smack Down. "Sis', you' tell him?" He asked.

"Oh yea, Smack. My brother need five of my ki's. He got a sale fo' 'em," America said.

"Aaagh," Smack Down was a little reluctant.

"Fam', I been doin' this. My people can't go without just because you came aboard." Ren made it seem like his sister was doing him a favor when in fact, Smack Down was doing them a justice. But five kilos wasn't nothing. Smack Down would really be getting seventy-five kilograms and stretching them to ah hundred and twenty-five bricks. So her cut wouldn't change, but instead of 1.2 million dollars, he would be making 2.8 million.

"I feel you. I'll make my call. Once I grab up, I'll text you and tell you where to come and pick the five up at."

"Cool," Ren said shaking his head.

"Thanks again, Smack Down," America said putting her arms out for a hug. Before Smack Down hugged America, he looked down at her hard nipples pointing through her wife-beater. She seen his eyes looking at them. She embraced him tightly, letting him know that she wanted him to do more than look.

"Ayo, and thanks fo' yesterday. Lookin' out fo' my sis'. I don't know what I would I've done without her." Ren said.

"No doubt. Now let me get outta here, and get on this. My man just gotta load in. He waiting to see if the fifty bricks is ah go."

"Damn, ya man got it like that? On deck like that?" Ren asked. Not thinking about what he was saying.

"Hell yeah. We good," Smack Down said hating everything about Ren.

"Let me walk you out," America offered. Outside, she hugged Smack Down again. This time she gave him a kiss on the cheek after hugging him. "Please, be careful. I don't want nothing to happen to my li'l Jigga."

"Ya Jigga?" Smack Down said putting the night bag filled with five-hundred thousand dollars into his van. He walked around to the driver's side, jumped into the van, started it up, and rolled down the passenger side window.

"Yea Smack, you my money getta like Jigga, I'm ya Bey," America answered.

"Oh yea?" Smack Down felt a similar connection to her. It reminded him of what he and Money had early in their relationship. "I'll be aight. This is what I do." He told her.

"Hit me when everything is done. Maybe we can get together for ah drink or something. Do it fo' the show or fo' real." America took her shot.

"Eh'thang I do is fo' real. But I don't know 'bout goin' out wit' you. You gotta stalker hitting you up wit' paint balls an' shit," Smack Down said jokingly.

"Yea right. Quit playin' wit' me. That bitch don't want no mo' problems. Especially after last night."

"What happened last night? You mean to tell some mo' action happened after I dropped ya ass off?" Smack Down asked leaning towards the passenger side.

"Yeeeaah! My brother beat da shit outta the two bodyguards that hit me up."

"Get da fuck outta here!"

"Hell yea!"

"Yo! Please tell me you ain't tell him 'bout that body."

"I tell him eh' thang, we don't keep secrets from each other ..."

"Aw maaan, what the fuck."

"But he ain't gonna say shit. That nigga put in work too. He was in the military. How you think that nigga that shot my mom's ended up dead down at the County?"

"He did that shit?"

America gazed at Smack Down for a couple of seconds. "He had it done."

"Daaamn! That reminds me, I gotta deal wit' that body." Smack Down said, cool and casual, like murder wasn't nothing to hi., He was remorseless.

"And I gotta go pick my moms up. She get out today, and I know she wanna know about everything that's goin' on."

"Aw, so you gon tell her too? This is crazy."

"If I don't my brother will. Nigga, we ain't no rats! You good. You saved my life. My people ain't gon' come at you with that snitch shit!" America started getting frustrated. Realizing that she may have fucked up her chances of getting with him. She knew that niggas didn't like nosey bitches or bitches that ran their mouths. Especially about murder.

"It's cool. I ain't trippin'." Smack Down lied. Now he was having second thoughts about saving her. If he killed his man, he should have killed her too.

"I couldn't tell her shit at the hospital. She thought the room was bugged."

"Damn, she be noided like that?"

"I told you we know all about the game."

"You don't know nothin', I'm out," Smack Down said putting his van into drive.

"Be safe, my li'l Jigga." She taunted him.

"Whateva." Smack Down said pulling off. America gave him some things to think about. He thought about having all three of the Duvalls killed. He didn't like the fact that they knew about what he did. Then he thought about what proof they would have. "NONE!" He said out loud and shook the thought of killing America out of his head. Then he thought about her brother beating Dominican

Flames' body guards up. Them some big niggas, he thought to himself. "Nigga's ah five brick headache, all in the fuckin' way." He thought. "I'll have CNN bring him five joints we already got cut up." He told himself out loud. "Should I do it before the big deal? Nah, can't risk CNN, I don't know what this clown's up to. We do it ah hour after we put eh' thang up, just in case he tries something," he thought.

HAND OF THE DEAD BODY

At the home of Detective Castadena Gordy a phone call interrupted Detective Gordy's sleep. "Hello?" Detective Gordy answered her cell phone, groggy and half asleep.

"Get up. We gotta stiff in a studio on McKnight Road. Looks like the victim's linked to that reality show we work for," Detective Ray Burnam told his Robbery Homicide Division partner.

"What? Another cast member? Did you call the producers of the show?" She asked.

"Yup, before I called you. Sorry, babe, money first."

"Ray, don't be sorry. That's what she's paying us for. So her camera people are on their way over there?" Detective Gordy was speaking of Money King's camera crew. The two detectives had made a deal with the producers of Love & Trap Muzik, Pittsburgh. They were to give any firsthand information about the Sexy Duvall case to them in exchange for money. With that case closed, the detectives seen other opportunities that evolved around the new victim of the show.

As she finished washing her face, Detective Gordy's partner called again. "Yea Ray?" She answered her cell phone.

"Today is our lucky day. Another body and guess what? It's tied to Love & Trap Muzik, Pittsburgh."

"You gotta be kiddin'," Detective Gordy said checking her dark complected face for any sleep that may have been left in the corners of her eyes.

"Nope." Detective Burnam answered. It's no joke. It's the third stiff tied to the show."

"You made the call?" Detective Gordy asked.

"Yup. They're sending out a second camera crew. You head over there. I'll take the one on McKnight Road."

"Where am I going?"

"3-1-9 Balboa." Detective Burnam gave Detective Gordy the address to the home of the third victim related to the Pittsburgh based reality show.

***

Bass-Line Recording Studio, 1021 McKnight Road.

"What are we looking at here. Run me through it," Detective Burnam requested of a Medical Examiner Technician.

"Execution-style murder. One to the back of the head and another to make sure the victim was dead." The tech told the RHD detective.

"Typical street thug killin'. Shit, they watch this shit on TV. They leave no witnesses or they make sure he's dead, shit. They imitate it in the deadliest ways," Detective Burnam said looking at the remains of Carson "Hitter B" Wells. He took notes as he watched the medical examiner work the scene.

The soundboard, notepad, and soundproof walls were all covered with skull and brain fragments. A shiny black vinyl body bag laid unzipped beside Hitter B awaiting his cold, lifeless body to enter it.

Technicians methodically took pictures, blood samples, and documented everything worth value on the scene. LTMP cameramen videotaped what they were allowed to. Monte Bucks planned to get pictures of Hitter B's body at the morgue. He had contacted his family and propositioned them. He would take care of all funeral expenses in exchange for photos of the body.

Detectives Burnam and Gordy also accepted fees for inside information about the murder and were to make statements for the show.

"Give me something," Detective Burnam said in an emotionless monotone to another tech taking pictures of the murder scene.

"Aaagh, it's a lot going on here. But what I can say for now is that this was a well thought out murder. At one point the floor was covered with something. And the victim trusted whoever shot him…"

"Hold up. You said the floor had been covered?" Detective asked making sure he heard the tech correctly.

"Yes. You have blood on the soundboard, notepad, everything but the floor. The way this man's body is positioned isn't the position it was in when he first fell to the floor. Put it this way whoever shot him placed something underneath the victim before shooting them, possibly a sheet of plastic or something. And after he shot him, instead of rolling the body up and moving it, he pulled whatever material it was from underneath the victim causing him to roll into the position we found him in."

"So I need to check every garbage bend in the vicinity?" Detective Burnam asked.

"For starters," the tech said taking a few more pictures of Hitter B's body. He was also on Monte Bucks' payroll.

"Hmph, wow!" Detective Burnam shook his head.

"Let me continue to gather what I can and I'll keep you informed," the tech told the detective.

"Please do," Detective Burnam said.

"Oh! But let me remind you that this is a studio so there will be a lot of DNA samples of innocent people rendered. People walk in and out of here a thousand times a day. So get ready to do a lot of work," the tech advised.

Second crime scene, 319 Balboa

Fighting through the small crowd of uniformed officers, news crew lights, cameras and spectators, Detective Gordy scribbled her initials on a line of the crime scene attendance log, and ducked up under the yellow crime scene tape.

Placing her *Ulyana Sergrenko* hand embroidered sunglasses on top of her head, she held the back of her hand to her mouth and nose. The stench of the dead body was strong.

"Anything good for me?" She asked a Medical Examiner Technician watching another dusting the fingerprints poder onto the knob of the front door.

"Victim's cell phone. It's been ringing non-stop."

A message alerted. Detective Gordy took the LCD screen on the phone and read fifty-nine missed calls. "What else," Detective Gordy asked.

KINGDOMS OF RUINS

At the Devall Estate, America and Ren helped their mother into the house, up the steps, and into her bedroom. Inside were flowers, balloons, gifts, and get well cards. "Ren, get this shit outta here."

"Maaa!" America couldn't believe what she was hearing from her mother. She thought that she would be happy to see all the love people had for her.

"America, I'm sick of looking at this type of shit. All it does is remind me of that damn hospital, and that I've been shot the fuck up. I don't need to look at this shit for that. I got all these bullet wounds, and scars for that!"

"Calm down, ma. I got you. I understand. Let's just get you into the bed, and Ren will get this stuff outta here," America said. "Yea. I got you, ma." Ren said as he started removing the gifts.

"Thank you, baby. Ugh…Agh, shiiit! This shit hurts. Staples and stitches an' all this shit. I feel like Frankenstein's bride an' shit. Did GQ send me anything," Sexy Duvall asked getting into the bed.

"I thought you didn't want this stuff." "Bitch, did he send me some'in'?"

"Yes ma."

"What?"

"Like ten dozen roses, that's them right there." America pointed at the roses DQ Dawg sent. "You wanna read the card?" America asked.

"Yea. Let me see it. Aaagh, shit!" Sexy Duvall felt pain up and down her body every time she moved. Pain was written all over her face.

"It says…" America played like she was going to read the card.

"I can read it! Let me see it." Sexy Duvall demanded.

THE CARD READ:

To the realest woman I know.

Love you, and I can't wait 'til you fully recovered so you can

get back to running shit!

Love GQ

"Aw, that bullshit. Reennnn!" Sexy Duvall called out to her son.

"Yea ma?" He answered.

"I want some Olive Garden. You feel like getting me some?"

"Yea ma. I got you. What you want?" Ren asked stepping back into his mother's bedroom to remove more of her flowers and gifts.

"Get me that Tour of Italy. I'm try'na eat."

"Aight. I'll be back," he said kissing his mother on her forehead. "Love you," he stated before leaving out to go get her food.

"Love you too, soldier." Sexy Duvall said calling Ren by the nickname she had given him. When he had come home from the military.

"You want me to get you anything now, ma?" America asked.

"Ah glass of wine and ah blunt." Sexy Duvall said with a serious look on her face.

"Maaa!"

"Americaaah! Don't play, bitch! Roll da fuck up. I need something to take my mind off of this pain."

"Kay. I got you."

"Where's my phone. Did the lawyer get it back?"

"Yea, I got it in da safe. Monte got some serious mouthpieces on his payroll. Our lawyer couldn't get it back. His lawyer made one phone call, and they released it back to us," America said.

"Yea, Monte got power. He's the most powerful black man in Pittsburgh, legal-wise, and one of the most powerful men in the entertainment industry."

"Shit! He cut ah million-dollar check like it wasn't shit. Made me think I should've asked for more."

"I know that's right, baby girl," Sexy laughed.

"For real. Let me get ya stuff fo' you, ma. You wanna see the pictures from the Teaser Party?" America asked her mother as she walked out her mother's bedroom into hers.

"Yea. Bring them too. I loved the Teaser!" Sexy Duvall replied adjusting herself into a comfortable position.

"YEA, WE KILLED THAT. WE GOT OVER 40 MILLION VIEWS ON YOUTUBE!" America yelled from her room. She punched a combination of numbers into the electronic keypad on her safe that was hidden behind a large family portrait, hanging on her bedroom wall. 1-2-0-4 unlocked it. Inside was two-hundred thousand dollars, her mother's cell phone inside of a sealed evidence bag, her mother's black book, and client ledger.

America took out her mother's cell phone and ledger, then locked her safe back up. Grabbing the Teaser Party pictures off of her dresser, she looked around to see if she was leaving anything. Spotting her *Lanvin* bag, she grabbed it and headed back to her mother's bedroom.

"I brought you ya black book and ledger too." America said, sitting everything on her mother's bed.

"Thank you, princess. I know them trick ass ma'fuckas was goin' crazy when they thought I was goin' to die. You know ya mom got the best pussy on planet earth," Sexy Duvall said.

"Ma, you-are-currr-raaae-zee!"

"America, roll up!" Sexy Duvall demanded. She had not smoked since she had gotten shot. "Aaagh, America. Be careful!" Sexy Duvall said. America caused her pain when she climbed on her bed.

"Sorry, ma." America said digging into her purse and pulling a baby food jar filled with Sour Diesel out of it.

Sexy Duvall opened the packet of pictures and took them out of their picture envelope. The first picture she saw was a picture of America, Beyoncé and Jay Z. "DAMN!" She expressed with disappointment.

"What, ma?" America asked stuffing a blunt with Sour.

"I'm mad as hell I couldn't be there."

"Yea, I wish you could have been there, too." America licked the blunt leaf and tightly wrapped it around the Sour.

"Shit! Jay and Bey! I would've got in their bed for free."

"You crazy, ma." America told her mother again. She lit the blunt, took a few puffs and passed it to her mother.

"I see y'all was kickin' drip," Sexy Duvall said.

217

"Ma, they some real ma'fuckas." America said about Jay Z and Bey.

"They gettin' that paper, too." Sexy Duvall said looking closely over the picture.

"I got me ah money getta," America announced.

"Girl, who?"

"Whyyyy?"

"Bitch! Who!"

"Smack Down."

"Girl, you can't handle that nigga. Besides that, that's my girl's baby daddy. Aaaannnd she's the one that hired you to be on the show. Do you really wanna play ya'self like that?" Sexy Duvall gave her daughter something to think about. "I need to call Money. That's my bitch. I'll cut ya ass about her…"

"Whateva!" America rolled her eyes at her mom.

"You think cause he saved ya life, and he flippin' ya money, he's yours? He's always goin' to be Money's. She lost her legs because of him. That's why he don't get along wit' Mr. Frosty..."

"Why, ma?" America had told her mom about some of the things that were going on while she was in the hospital. Now she wanted the tea on Smack Down, and the executive producer of the show, Ms. Money King.

"Smack Down got Money caught up in ah jack move he did and after Money had their son, she got shot by the brother of the dude they jacked. Mr. Frosty tried to kill Smack Down, shot his ass up..."

"Whhhaaat!"

"Hell yea. They wanted to put Mr. Frosty in jail, but Smack Down wouldn't testify against him. So he ah stand up nigga. But like I was saying, he dedicated his life to her. He's always at her beck and call. Look, I don't wanna tell you that he's outta ya league, but princess, they're outta ya league. Shit! I ain't even in Money's league. I wouldn't be surprised if that work you copping today was coming from her. She been getting money just as long as Smack Down

219

has been. And she got connections. For real, for real, this is her fuckin' show."

"Damn! I ain't know all ah that," America said, watching her mother hit the blunt and go to the next picture. "Is that nigga that kidnapped you in here?" Sexy Duvall wanted to see the dead man that had kidnapped her daughter.

"Yea, let me see." America took the stack of pictures and flipped threw them until she came to a picture of Smack Down and the late Hitter B. *"Shut up, bitch! Shut up, fo' I kill ya ass!"* America could still her Hitter B's voice as she relived the ordeal in her head.

"That's him?" Sexy Duvall asked.

"Yea, that's him." America answered with tears in her eyes.

"Aaaw princess, you ain't gotta worry 'bout him no more, he's gone. What I am worried about is you and Dominican. We need to put an end to y'all feud. If she gotta beef it should be with me, not you. I'm the one that got the footage. What's her number?" Sexy Duvall said asking for Dominican Flames' phone number.

America looked in her bag for her phone. "Damn, I must've left my phone in the car."

"Let me get it outta my phone."

"I'm gonna get mine," America said walking out to get her cell phone.

"Aight, ere, you want this?" Sexy Duvall extended her arm with the blunt in her hand.

"Nah, I'll roll another one when I get back."

Sexy Duvall tore the clear plastic bag her cell was in. Reading the word, "Evidence", that was stamped on the side of it. After turning her phone on, colorful designs and logos went across the screen. She waited a few seconds and then her sim-card unlock screen popped up. She punched 6-3-7-2 into the screen, and her phone unlocked.

"Uh…Uh…Uh, shit!" America ran backed into the house out of breath bypassing her seven missed calls to get to Dominican Flames' number.

"I can't believe you and Dominican are beefin'. That bitch is 'pose to be our manager." Sexy Duvall said, going to her call log, but as she did her message alerts started popping up on her LCD screen with continuity. "FUCK! These damn messages keep poppin' up." Then she paused for a second when she saw the number of her jackers still in her phone.

"Fuck that bitch. She ain't my fuckin' manager, you is. Here go her number."

"Dial it," Sexy Duvall said.

"She might not answer when she sees my number," America replied.

"You right, let me call her from my phone. She'll definitely answer that."

America's phone vibrated and she quickly answered it. "Hello…Two people…When? That's crazy. I'm sorry to hear that."

"Hello? Hi Dominican, I'm glad to be home. Look we need to talk…Ah detective? For what? Oh, okay. That's crazy. Call me soon as you can. I'ma try to hit ya mom and pops. After nine…Okay…Love you too." Sexy Duvall had called Dominican Flames so she could kill the beef between the two girls that had grew up like sisters.

Dominican Flames told her to come to her club after nine, and she would set up a call with her parents for her. Sexy Duvall had their numbers but since her shooting their numbers had been changed. She also had told her that one of her men had been murdered, and she was sitting there with a detective.

"Sounds good. We'll be here at the house," America told her caller.

"Who's that?" Sexy Duvall asked.

"It's show time for you. That was the cameraman from the show. They try'na get some footage. They want to reenact you coming home from the hospital."

"I'm not goin' back to that fuckin' hospital!" Sexy Duvall said. Her message alerts were still going off.

"No ma, just you getting out the car coming into the house. Ah couple other shots of us talkin', you know?"

"Oh Okay. Hey, one of Dominican's men got killed last night. She said he got shot. I thought you said Soldier just fought those guys last night."

"He did. He didn't shoot nobody last night. But that's what the cameraman was tellin' me. They were just coming from the murder scenes of two men associated with cast members from the show. We know one was my kidnapper, but guess who her man was that got shot?"

"Who?"

"Pedro, that security guard that sold us the footage."

"See, that's why this shit gotta end. Cause I'm already dealin' wit' losin' ya grandma, and I'm not try'na lose you or ya brother over this bullshit. Cause the Crouch goes hard. That's who prolly got Pedro killed from his jail cell." Sexy Duvall was talking about Dominican Flames' father, Peter "Brooklyn Pete" Duarte.

WHO GOT THE JUICE

At the female correctional center in Hazelton, WV., Giselle "El Grunona" Duarte, stood on the second tier of her cell block with a few of her female goons around her. She was the shot caller of the Latin Americans in the facility. Her and her husband, Brooklyn Pete Duarte, had been locked up for twenty-one years. They had put in for clemency several times, and had been denied time and time again.

With Congressional attempts to restore sentencing discretion judges, and the fairness in Cocaine Sentencing Act in 2009, they had received some relief, but still had over a decade left in their sentences.

When the bill abolished the heightened penalties and mandatory minimums for drug offenses involving cocaine based cases, such as crack cocaine, they both believed that they would be immediately released, but that wasn't the case.

Her long stay in prison had kept her angry and mad. This is why they called her "Grunona," it meant grouch in Spanish. At first her friends called her that in secrecy. When she heard about the nickname she didn't like it, but her husband found it to be cute so she grew to accept it.

Grunona, gazed out at the cells and inmates surrounding her and felt sick. She was sick of doing time. Sick of watching the same activities taking place every day; the card and domino playing, the working out, and the same TV programs. It was close to six o'clock, and she and her bandillera's stood in the same place they did everyday around that time waiting for mail-call. La Patrona de Patronas and her mafia, "La Senora's del Bandida's", watched as the C.O. running the block walked in the Unit with the mail carrier pouch.

"MAIL CALL!" He yelled out. He poured the mail out on a table in the unit as inmates gathered around him, waiting to see if they got mail. After a few seconds he picked pieces of mail up, read the name on the envelope, and called it out.

"BALVIN...PALMER...SANTOS...DUARTE...D
UARTE...DUARTE...DUARTE...DUARTE!" The
inmate that ran the block for her, Kieko Silverio, grabbed
Grunona's mail and brought it to her.

"Gracias," Grunona told her right-hand bitch,
accepting her mail.

"What time you want ya phone?" Kieko asked the
lady O.G.

"Right after nine o'clock count," Grunona said.

"Some lady named, Sexy, called you." Kieko told
her in Spanish, about an illegal cell phone and Sexy Duvall
calling.

"SEXY?! Awww, that's my bitch! What she say?"

"I told her you weren't available, and I would let
you know that she called.

"Okay, I'll call her after nine. I'ma go lay down for
a minute."

"Okay, I got the girls bagging up the work, and it should be ready to put out tonight."

"Good, stay on top of it. Who works tonight?" Grunona asked.

"Our girl, C.O. Bradley."

Grunona nodded her head then went inside of her cell to relax.

Inside, Grunona sat on her bunk and laid her mail on the bed. There were several pieces; two cards, an envelope of pictures, a Pittsburgh Tribune, and a Vanity Affair with Monte Bucks on the cover.

Lying back in her bunk, Grunona picked up the Vanity Affair and flipped through the pages until she saw the cover article on her daughter, Dominica "Dominican Flames" Duarte's, boss. She had heard about Monte Bucks, but knew little about him. She hoped that the article would enlighten her about the billionaire her daughter worked for.

MONTE BUCKS' VANITY AFFAIR ARTICLE:

Monte, Bucks stands inside of the boardroom where he conducts most of his business meetings. Several feet away from the plush chairs and boardroom table he holds court. He's staring out of a tall wall of glass at the sprouting water fountain inside of Pittsburgh's Point State Park puffing on a Davidoff Blend with two massive Presa Canarios on each side of him. They were awaiting his every command as were his assistants standing around with clipboards and his camera crew holding giant lights, shooting our interview for his reality TV show, Love & Trap Muzik, Pittsburgh.

Normally, the billionaire with his collection of two million dollars in cars, is encircled by a fashionable international crowd made up of top-name

Hip-Hop and R&B artist, producers, animation artist, muses, politicians, and media moguls, gathered for two thousand dollar shots of Louis XIII in the courtyard of the palace he calls, 'Bucks Plaza Hotel.

As a key figure and part of an international elite group of industrialist, heiresses, and playboys, he ping-

ponged across the Atlantic, surfing global skies in luxurious Gulf Stream Jets the province of moviemakers.

Born in 1962 to a runaway teenage mother that gave him away to his grandparents, Monte Bucks, pursued a singing career at an early age, pitching his demo to whomever would listen. In the early 80's he cashed his first million-dollar check, and led one of music's most influential groups. Topping the charts with worldwide hits like, "Let Me Lace My Joint with You" and a dance groove called "If He Can Have You, I Can Too." But after its second tour, financial differences between the band members, the Pittsburgh based group, broke apart.

Not one to be stifled, Bucks took two thousand dollars and cofounded Chalice Recordings with the group's keyboardist, "Jimmy 'Funky Fingers' Count, and they went on to write and produce smash hits that turned their record label into a multi-million-dollar company. After signing a one hundred-million-dollar distribution deal with Sony and expanding it with an ancillary brand, like Mega-Bucks gaming.

In 1997, with two platinum albums, and a dozen Grammys, he made a decision to leave the music industry. He sold his half of the company for $400 million, and invested in film and television production.

In 1998, using his entrepreneurial mentality he partnered with Lionsgate and helped start Animax, and an animation company that linked some of the world's highest paid artists to do the voice overs of some of the movie industry's most famous animated characters.

Using film and television as a platform, he purchased his own 200,000 square foot studio, and wrote, produced, and directed his first Blockbuster movie.

According to Forbes, this year the Fortune 500 CEO's estimated worth is somewhere around 1.8 Billion, and now with 30 years of movie and music knowledge, the Pittsburgh native and visionary, has singlehandedly placed his city on the reality television map. Giving the new generation of Pittsburgh artists a chance to spotlight their talents on the reality television he co-created, Love & Trap Muzik, Pittsburgh.

When I stepped inside of the boardroom, the singer-mogul, shook my hand, and invited me to take a seat at the table he made most of his multi-million dollar deals at. Saturating his palate with the smoke of the Davidoff, he reclined in a chair that resembled a throne, fit for a king, ready to relive his life for this interview.

This being the first time meeting the lord of various business ventures, I studied his slender athletic build, bald head, and angular face.

"I had my staff bring ya Smart Water. If you want something stronger then that let me know." He said gazing at me through a cloud of scented smoke. Before him laid an ashtray, v-cutter, and a tablet in a leather embroidered case.

"No thanks. This is fine," I lied. I wouldn't have minded a two thousand dollar shot of Louis, and one of them beyond-gorgeous supermodels he so often paraded around the world with. Instead we were in the company of bobble headed assistants, cameramen, and two man-eaters called The Dot and The Dub.

"So let's get on with it," he said, leaning back as he stroked his close shaven, salt-and-pepper goatee with one hand and his expensive torpedo in the other.

Pushing my water to the side, I pressed record on my iPhone 6, and asked the first question to the black business man dressed in a shirt and suit that emphasized quality fabrics, and tailoring I was sure came from the Perkens Bien Aime Collection.

VA: So what can we expect from season two of Love & Trap Muzik, Pittsburgh?

MB: A lot of entertainment! A lot of action! Live footage from a murda investigation, grudge fights, performances from the cast members and mega-stars. The whole works. We bringing it on another level.

VA: 30 years in the industry is a long time. Have you ever thought about publishing a memoir?

MB: That's actually in the works. One of the guys from the show, GQ Dawg, is co-writing it with me.

He just signed a publishing deal with my new publishing company, Bucks Baby Publishing. He ran the ideal at me, and I was all for it. I believe it's time for me to tell my story.

VA: You were part of the group Status in the eighties, and found success with the group. But due to financial differences the group split. Have you ever thought about doing a reunion tour?

MB: To date, Status, has sold 20 million records. We could have sold 100 million, but it wasn't meant to be. We all moved on. A reunion, I doubt it. It's not in my plans. We've had private jam sessions, but that just not something I'm interested in.

VA: Shortly after the split, you started your own record label, Chalice Recordings. But in 1997 you sold your part of the company, and walked away from the music business. Why was that?

MB: I felt like the music industry, not the music was declining. So I walked away while I was still on top. A state of independence was on the rise. Artist like Puffy, Jay Z, Cash Money Records, Aftermath and several others were coming in the game to reset the scoreboard. So I just got outta their way. I just felt that my era in the music industry had ran its course.

VA: You quit during the time some would say was the golden era of the industry 1988-2003. But you didn't stop developing artists.

Some of the artist you just mentioned are some of the artists you helped become successful, do you take responsibility for that?

MB: That's a tricky question. How do you take claim to that? How do you take responsibility for the success of an artist that's already successful?

Yes, I've given a lot of advice to upcoming artist. I've given them advice at 3:00 A.M., and I still do.

Me and Dre have spent hours discussing the future of Hip Hop, but I'm not looking for a pat on the back. I'm not asking an hourly fee. I'm not a blood-sucking lawyer. I just tell them what I believe is best for them at the time.

VA: Is that what you do with the cast members of LTMP?

MB: That's exactly how I handle things with my family members. Love & Trap Muzik, Pittsburgh is a show I co-created with my partner, Money King. We've created an outlet for young artist to display their talent.

But their drive, their story makes millions of viewers relate to them and believe in them. And that's what makes them successful. It's just my advice that keeps them successful.

"Patrona…Patrona, they just showed it on the news. Pedro is dead. We got him." Kieko ran to Grunona's cell to tell her that the hit she put out on the security guard that crossed her daughter had been carried out.

Grunona sat back and closed her eyes. She thought about the day she would run a Fortune 500 company and make the Forbes list like Monte Bucks.

MONEY & POWER

On the way to Reflection's Night Club, Sexy Duvall spoke to Giselle Duarte, in Spanish. "I know girl. I'm sorry about how that shit got handled." Sexy Duvall said.

"And I'm sorry about Dominica recording Ren's fight and selling it to the show. She crazy. I don't understand what's going on with these two. They were raised as sisters," Grunona said.

"It's this damn reality show. Got everybody going crazy. And Monte…"

"Monte Bucks?" Giselle asked.

"Yea, his ass talking 'bout he glad they deadin' the beef. He said he got homicide detectives breathing down his neck, and protesters threatening to shut the show down. it's crazy, girl." Sexy Duvall told Giselle about what Monte Bucks was saying about the show.

"Homicide? What they say, Sexy?"

"Nothin' much. They think that some serial killer type of ma'fucka's running around killin' reality show ma'fuckas."

"What? Eh'body 's crazy out there. Maybe I should keep my ass in here, girl," Grunona said.

"Yea right! Bitch, I need ya ass out here!" Sexy Duvall said to her close friend. Just like their daughters, they had grown up calling each other sisters. For Grunona to laugh was out of the norm. Hearing her playfully joke was not something her bandillera's were used to. Giselle had earned her name "The Grouch" honestly. And for someone to call her bitch was completely unheard of inside the Federal Correctional Center. Many had died for less. Your tone of voice could get you killed. There was only one person she loved, feared and submitted to, and that was her husband, Brooklyn Pete. He wasn't as deadly as his wife, but definitely more powerful.

"So when are they lettin' ya ass out girl?" Sexy Duvall asked.

"Me and Pete just put in for clemency again. Obama has been showing love. He let close to two hundred people go. We're hoping that our case hits his desk, and he releases us." Grunona told Sexy Duvall.

***

"Hello?" America answered her phone, it was Ren calling her. "What's up, brother?"

"Hey, I'm on my way to meet'cha man. "

"By yourself right?" America asked.

"Come on, A'!"

"BY YOURSELF. RIGHT?!" America said catching her mother's eye. They were simultaneously having conversations.

"Yea A', by myself." Ren wanted to take Hooker, but America wouldn't allow him to.

"We're goin' to *FACETIME* Pete. He wants to talk to the girls together," Grunona stated.

"Bye brother. Call me when you make it back safe." America said to Ren ending their conversation.

"I guess he's gonna make 'em kiss and make up." Sexy Duvall continued her conversation.

"Bitch! They better not fuck that money up cause I'm sick of funding Dom's little business ventures."

"You! I'm so glad America's gettin' her own money now."

Grunona laughed.

"For real, Giselle, girl." Sexy Duvall looked over at her daughter. "Hey, we're about to be pulling up, I will call you soon, and I will definitely be praying for you and my brother's release. Shit! I might have to go suck the President's dick, or have ah threesome with him and Michelle's fine ass to get y'all out. You know I will."

America looked over at her mother and chuckled. "Maaa! "

Grunona laughed. "Bitch do whatever you gotta do. Just get us up out this bitch!"

"Sis', I got y 'all. Hey I'm gon'. Love You with eh' thang in me, senora del bandida."

I Need A Bawss In My Life

"Love you, too, doll face," Grunona said pressing end on her smartphone. As she leaned back.

Kieko watched her boss, and after a few seconds she asked, "Who was that?"

"One of the realest bitches I've ever known in my life," Grunona answered.

***

At the Pittsburgh Inn, somewhere on Route 65, Ren was pulling into the parking lot. Little did he know he was being tailed by two money hungry detectives, Gordy and Burnam. They had already made fifty thousand that day and were looking to make more. The more money they made off of providing information to Monte Bucks, the more they wanted. It was easy money. After receiving the fifty-thousand-dollar payment, Burnam had come up with an idea.

"Why don't we put the cast members of LTMP under surveillance? All of these luxury cars, diamonds and mansions, they gotta be doing something illegal. I say we follow 'em and if we catch 'em doin' something illegal, we

241

bust they asses. But instead of arresting them and them getting out on a hundred- thousand-dollar bail, we just sell them back to Monte Bucks for half of the price. They never get arrested and we get paid." He told his partner.

Detective Gordy thought that it was a great idea and was all for it. They searched *Facebook*, *Instagram* and *Twitter* accounts for anything that would lead them to their first victim, which was America Duvall.

After reviewing America' s media pages, listening closely to her lyrics, and seeing her with Jay Z, they believed if they were caught doing something wrong it would lead to a huge payday. So after doing a background check, they had found out where she lived and when they saw her pulling out of her estate driveway, they followed her. But the only thing was the person behind the tinted windows of the luxury vehicle listed in America Duvall's name was Ren not her. But the two detectives didn't realize that until they saw him get out of the C-class coupe.

"Who in da fuck is that?" Detective Gordy asked her partner.

"I don't know. The more important question is, what's in that bag he's carrying?" Detective Burnam said, eyeing the bag Ren was carrying.

"Looks empty," Detective Gordy said.

"He's here to fill it up. I wonder who's behind that door," Detective Burnam said with his hand on the car door lever.

"Let's wait till he gets in there, then kick the door in. We don't need no warrant for what we're doin', and if he makes us, let's kill his ass and whoever's in there waiting," detective Gordy said.

"It ain't like we can't get away with it. All we gotta say is we're following a lead, and when we see the suspect kick in the door we protected and served," detective Burnam laughed.

***

Inside room 106 at Pittsburg Inn Smack Down stood looking out of his hotel room window. "This idiot pulls up in ah fuckin' C-class to pick up five ki's. What the fuck?" Smack Down said talking to CNN on his cell phone.

"Looks like he brought company with him," CNN said.

"You bullshittin'! Duuumb muthafucka, man!" Smack Down couldn't believe that Ren had brought the cops to him.

"He's about to knock on the door..." CNN told Smack Down.

KNOCK! KNOCK! KNOCK! KNOCK!

Smack Down killed the lights and opened the door for Ren. "GET IN HERE! You bought the fuckin' cops with you!" Smack Down said through clenched teeth.

"WHAT?! I AIN'T BRING NO PO-PO WIT' ME!"

"Shut the fuck up, and help me move these joints to the other room," Smack said to Ren, furious. "Fuckin' po-po! Who even talks like that anymore?!" He thought to himself picking up four of the five kilos. "Grab that one," he told Ren, holding his cell phone to his ear with his shoulder.

"THEY'RE COMIN' TO THE DOOR! GET THE FUCK OUTTA THERE, SMACK!" CNN warned Smack.

"THEY'RE COMIN'! HURRY UP!" Smack Down said to Ren, more mouthing it than saying it out loud. He didn't want the police to hear his voice.

Ren picked up the fifth kilo, and made it to the door that led to the adjoining room, but it was too late.

Detective Burnam kicked the motel room door in. "GET DOWN! GET ON THE FLOOR! GET ON THE FLOOR!" Ren did as he was told.

Detective Gordy turned on the lights. Ren looked at the door that led to his escape. It was closed. Hearing the police at the door that lead to the other room, Smack Down closed and locked it.

Outside, CNN, waited for the detectives to close the door they had kicked in and drove slowly up to the room

Smack Down was in. "Come on, Smack, I'm out front," CNN said.

Smack Down ran out of the room and jumped in CNN's car with an overnight bag with the four kilo's in it.

"Nigga, you crazy!" CNN said quickly pulling off.

"I wasn't leaving this shit. That stupid ma'fucka lost is my gain!" Smack Down said looking in back of him through the rearview mirror making sure that they weren't being followed.

"Yaw good now?" Sexy Duvall asked, looking at American and Dominican Flames. They were in Dominican Flames' office at Reflections. They had just gotten off of a conference call with Dominican Flames' father, Brooklyn Pete, from a cell at USP Canaan.

"Yea. We good," America said wiping tears from her eyes.

"Yea ma', we straight," Dominican Flames said extending her arms to hug America.

America stepped in to hug Dominican Flames." I'm sorry, sis'," she said.

"Love you, America." Dominican Flames said.

Sexy Duvall watched the two of them. The thought that she could have lost one of them because of some video footage brought tears to her eyes. Brooklyn Pete said some harsh words to both of them. He was hard on them, but they all agreed on what he was saying. "So now let's get back to this money, bitches." Sexy Duvall said making all of them laugh.

"Yea Smack?!" America turned away to answer her phone.

"YA DUMB ASS BROTHA GOT BUSTED! HE BROUGHT THE FUCKIN' POLICE TO ME!" Smack Down yelled into the phone.

"Hol' up, what?! What you mean? Where? Where the fuck is he, Smack?"

"WHERE? What you mean? I can't do shit, okay." The call disconnected.

"What happened America?" Sexy Duvall asked.

"Yea, what the fuck, sis'?" Dominican Flames asked.

"Ren got busted at ah motel on 65," America said sitting down, and putting her face in her hands.

"I told you about that nigga," Sexy Duvall said.

"SHUT UP, MA! IT WASN'T HIS FAULT! Ren was being followed and led the cops to him," America said.

"How the fuck did he get away and my son didn't?" Sexy Duvall asked.

"Ma, I don't know." America replied.

"I keep tellin' his ass he ain't no hustler. You goin' in ya stash to get him out. I ain't pay in' fo' that shit!"

"Ma, I ain't ask you to. I got this!" America said.

"I'll help you get his fine ass out. But he gotta do house arrest at my spot," Dominican Flames said with a serious look on her face.

America and her mother laughed.

***

"I know whatcha thinkin'. Ya thinkin', *I'm done, I'm not sayin' shit! How the fuck am I going to get outta this shit?* But we don't wanna put you in jail. We not try'na flip. Hell, we ain't even gon' take ya drugs. What the fuck we gon' do wit' that? All we want is fifty-thousand dollars, and you can go. You prolly could make that off that kilo sittin' beside you."

Ren looked down at the brick sitting by him.

"But unless you get us fifty-thousand within the next hour, you'll never get to sell that bitch," detective Burnam said.

"I can get that, hand me my phone," Ren told the detectives.

"Well, you'll get'cha chance. We gon' call billionaire Monte Bucks and let him take care of it fo' you. Then you can pay him back. We try'na impress him. Let him know how important it is to keep us around. I know the show y'all doin' is ah rap show, but I got ways to turn all you muthafuckas into singers," detective Gordy said.

"Man, let me get y'all this money so I can get up out this bitch," Ren said.

"Hold up! My partner's calling Bucks now," detective Gordy said.

Detective Burnam pulled out his cell phone, and called Monte Bucks' phone.

***

Outside of *Tadich Grill*, San Francisco, Monte Bucks and Money King were leaving. "I can't believe we flew all the way to San Francisco so you can eat at *Tadich*'s," Money said as she was elevated out of her wheelchair onto the blue/moccasin tan interior back seat of a midnight sapphire blue/seashell Rolls-Royce Phantom.

"What can I say, baby? I love Spicy Cioppino," Monte Bucks said to Money as he also climbed into the back seat from the opposite side of the Rolls-Royce.

Cioppino was a tomato-wine stew, brimming with clams, mussels, shrimp, whitefish, and Dungeness Crab. It came with a few slices of butter- soaked garlic bread made from *Boudin* sourdough and was prepared by Chef Wil Going.

"But El's just opened another Tadich Grill in D.C. we could have flown there instead of flying all the way to San Francisco, Monte," Money said trying to figure out the riddle in her head.

"Okay, you busted me. I wanted to be alone with you. Matter of fact, I want to spend the night with you and tomorrow before we fly home to Pittsburgh. We can stop and eat Szechuan shrimp and Mao Po Tofu specially prepared by our chef friend, Susanna Foo, in Philadelphia.

Money let what Monte was saying sink into her head. Then his cell phone rung. Money watched him as he studied the caller's name on the screen. "It's those pesky, money hungry cops again. Set ya phone to record this call, I really don't trust these muthafuckas. We need something to use against these muthafuckas whenever they decide to get outta hand," Monte Bucks told Money.

"Ready," Money said pressing record on her cell phone.

"Yes. What do you have for me this time?" Monte Bucks asked detective Burnam.

"We got one of ya guys, Renault Duvall, and a kilogram of pure white cocaine."

"Renault Duvall, that's not one of my guys. He's not on the show," Monte Bucks said looking over at Money to see if he was missing anything.

"That's Sexy's son. He's the one we got fighting Dominican's men," Money said whispering in Monte Bucks' ear.

"Yea...Yea...Yea, I know he's not on the show, but he's the brother of the main character on the show, America Duvall."

"Alright. So why'd you call me?" Monte Bucks asked.

"Well, I'm calling because I don't want the show catchi.ng no more heat before the second season starts. You

252

don't need to catch no more heat. You're already got three murders, a shooting, and now a kilogram of cocaine. All that plus a successful show, that shit sounds like a racketeering case waiting to happen. And we, me and my partner don't want to see you going through the hassle of no investigation, Mr. Bucks. Me and my partner, detective Gordy, love the show, don't we, Gordy?"

"We love the show, Mr. Bucks. It's great what'cha doin' fo' the kids." Monte Bucks and Money King looked at each other shaking their heads.

"So what do you suggest I do?" Monte Bucks asked.

"You pay us fifty-thousand, and we make this go away. It'll be like this never happened," detective Burnam said.

"You got it. I'll have one of my people call you within the hour."

"Thank you, Mr. Bucks. Nice doing business with you," detective Burnam said looking at detective Gordy with a smile on his face. Their plan had worked.

"Hey, can I speak to Renault?" Monte Bucks asked.

"Sure," detective Burnam handed his phone over to Ren, but before he could say a word, Money grabbed Monte Bucks' phone, and hung it up.

"We don't need you talking to him," she told Monte Bucks.

"Yea?" Ren said into a dead phone line. "The call must've dropped."

"Well, it's ya lucky day. But hey, do me a favor, and let us bust you again so we can charge Monte Bucks another fifty thousand or more. That ain't nothin' but a watch fee for that big time billionaire," detective Burnam said taking his phone back from Ren. Then the two detectives walked out of the crashed in motel room door.

"They might want you to pay fo' this," detective Gordy said, pointing at the door that was torn off of its hedges.

After Monte Bucks spoke to detective Burnam, Money called Sexy Duvall. The phone rung twice before Sexy Duvall answered.

***

At Reflection's night club Sexy answered her phone. "Hello?"

"Sexy, hi baby," Money's voice cut through the music playing in Sexy Duvall's background.

"HEY MONEY! I TRIED TO CALL YOU EARLY, GIRL!" Sexy Duvall said.

"Yea, I was outta town on business. I was going to call you tomorrow, but something urgent came up," Money said.

"What's goin' on?" Sexy Duvall asked.

"Where you at, ah club already? Your ass just got outta the hospital, Sexy," Money said.

"Like you said, somethin' urgent came up. Me and America's havin' drinks with Dominican. We're waitin' on an important call from my son, Ren."

"That's what I'm calling about, Sexy. He got busted with ah brick."

As Sexy Duvall and Money King were talking, Ren called his sister America' s phone. "BROTHER!" America yelled catching Dominican Flames and her mother's attention.

"At a motel. But Monte took care of everything, so he's not going to jail, and he's not going to be charged with anything. But you're going to have to make sure he leaves them drugs alone. The police mentioned a racketeering charge," Money said to Sexy.

"Oh, I'ma make sure of that. That muthafucka ain't no street nigga," Sexy said looking at America talking to her son. She was furious, and couldn't wait to talk to him. But she wasn't going to disrespect her friend and employer by cutting her call short.

"Oh, and Friday we're all getting together at Bucks' Plaza to watch the rough-edit of the first episode of the new show, so we want everyone there," Money said.

"THAT NIGGA SET ME UP!" Ren told America. Ren and America spoke to each other as Money and their mother spoke.

"Ren, what are you talkin' about? Why would he do that?" America defended Smack Down.

"I know he did. That shit happened too shady. That nigga was on his phone the whole time. He was talking to the fuckin' cops the whole time," Ren said hysterically.

"You sound crazy."

"Okay Sexy, I gotta go, and I know you need to holla at ya son, but I love you, and will definitely be over to see you when I get back in the 'burgh."

"Love you too, Money. Thanks, and tell Monte I said thanks, and I send my love," Sexy Duvall said to Money King before hanging up with her and snatching

America's phone from her. "BOY! WHAT THE FUCK HAPPENED?" She screamed into the phone.

"MA, THAT MUTHAFUCKA SET ME UP! I'MA DEAL WIT' THAT NIGGA!" Ren screamed back at his mother.

"YA ASS AIN' T DOIN' SHIT! YA NOT GONNA FUCK OUR MONEY UP REACTING TO YA SILLY AS THEORIES! WE DON'T NEED YOU GETTIN' US KICKED OFF OF THE SHOW, AND WE DEFINITLEY DON'T NEED NO FUCKIN' RACKETEERING CASE! No, where are you...No, don't come home they still might be on you. Go somewhere for tonight, and come home tomorrow…Kay, love you."

Listening to her mother yell at her brother about his stupidity, America thought about what her brother said. Even though she knew Smack Down would never set her brother up, especially with everything she knew about Hitter B's death. Thinking, she scrolled through her call log, and pressed her thumb on Smack Down's number. "THIS NUMBER HAS BEEN CHANGED OR IS NO LONGER IN SERVICE!" The recording echoed in her ear.

"What the fuck?" She thought wondering if she had just lost five-hundred thousand dollars.

PURPLE ONE STILL REIGN'S

As Monte Bucks' Falcon 7x flew from San Francisco to Philadelphia, he watched an episode of *Billionaire* on his LG 360 VR Glasses. "Baby, you gotta check these out, they 're incredible. I need to come up with something like this," Monte Bucks said to Money King, taking the virtual glasses off of his face and rested them on the top of his head. Then his cell phone rung. It was next to Money. She lounged on a plush leather recliner.

"See who that is. It better not be those pesky ass detectives," Money Bucks said putting his 360 VR's down and walking towards Money.

"It's not, it says, Tyka," Money said.

"Tyka? That's Prince's sister, answer that," Monte Bucks said reaching out for his phone. "Tyka?" Monte Bucks said into the cell phone, but there was silence so he looked to make sure she was on the line. "Tyka!" He called out again.

"He's gone, Monte," Tyka said in a low, dispirited voice. "What you mean he's gone? Who's gone? What are you talking about, Tyka?" Monte Bucks asked with worry starting to set in his voice. He felt weak, and took a seat on the edge of Money's recliner. He listened for a response.

Prince had told him that he had an emergency landing in Moline, Illinois, on the way home after doing a show April 14th. But decided to leave after the hospital could not compliment his stay. That night he had performed two shows, and did three encores. Two days after that, April 16th, Prince had called him, and invited him to a show he was having at Paisley, but Mon e Bucks had told him he was in another country on business and couldn't make it. It was that night that Prince had eerily told the crowd to "Wait a few days before wasting their prayer's on him.' So in Monte Bucks' mind, Tyka couldn't possibly be talking about her brother.

"Prince. My brother's dead, Monte."

"WHAT DO YOU MEAN HE'S DEAD? I just talked to him. NO! NO! Don't tell me no shit like that, Tyka! Is this some type of joke?" Monte Bucks' voice trembled. He didn't know how to respond to the heart stopping news. Tears poured from his eyes, his heart ached with grief.

Money rubbed his back. She couldn't hear what Tyka was saying, but she knew that Prince had passed from this life to the next by the look on Monte Bucks' face and his reaction. Slowly, she felt sadness overcome her and her body heated up. She lost control of her upper lip, and her nose burned as she began to cry also. She had only met Prince once at one of his charity events, but had known him all of her life through his music.

"We found him unresponsive on an elevator at Paisley," Tyka continued to tell Monte Bucks about her brother.

"You're shittin' me, Tyka!"

"No Monte, I wish I were. Hey, the police are on my other line. I gotta call you back."

"Tyka, please keep me posted. I'm on my way there," Monte said. "No. Just stay put until I sort everything out. Everything is so confusing right now," Tyka told Monte Bucks.

"What about his funeral? What do you need me to do?" Monte Bucks asked.

''He didn't want a funeral, Monte. We're going to have a private cremation service in a few days. I will keep you posted so you can attend. I know how close the two of you were. He loved you like a brother, I gotta go, but like I said, I'll keep you posted. Love you."

"Love you, too, I'm sorry, sis'. Truly I am," Monte Bucks said.

"Talk to you soon, doll," Tyka replied before clicking over to her other line.

Hearing how much Prince loved him really tore Monte Bucks up inside. Hundreds of people had seen him perform for the last time, had even seen his friend and brother do three encores, but because of business he wasn't there. "I wasn't there…I WASN'T THERE!" Monte Bucks said rocking back and forth. "He called me. Told me to come see him perform. Not once, but twice. I missed both times. He knew God was calling him home. Him and God were close, you know. God was all in his songs. He's in a place he wants to be, at Jehovah's side," Monte Bucks said. Money just listened to him, wiping tears from her eyes.

"Where's the remote, babe?" Monte Bucks asked Money.

"Right here," Money replied.

"Turn on *CNN*," Monte Bucks told her.

CNN:

"You've heard it here. The Breaking News has been confirmed. Music Icon, Prince, dead at age 57..."

"Oooh...Oh my god. Prince! PRRRIINNNCE!" Monte Bucks wailed falling back onto Money.

Money cried more, holding her new man. The night before they had decided to be a couple. She had grown tired of Smack Down and his crooked street ways. Him leaving her dinner to attend to the streets was the final straw. Now something had happened that had made her and Monte Bucks bond for life.

"This can't be real. It feels like a nightmare, Money. I just talked to him. He was mad that I couldn't make it to his last show. But we were out of the country."

"I know, baby. He forgives you," Money said comforting Monte Bucks.

"You want to hear my favorite song by him?"

"Yes, baby. What is it?" Money asked as Monte Bucks searched his phone for the song he loved the most by Prince.

"Everybody loves *Purple Rain, When Doves Cry and Let's Go Crazy*, my favorite is, *Sometimes It Snows In April.*" Monte Bucks pressed play on his phone, and the song began to play. Its guitar and piano played slow. The song was about a friend named Tracy. A friend that had died in a war. It spoke about death and love, and the snow that sometimes fell in April. *"Always cry for love, never cry for pain,"* one lyric was sung, *"I not afraid to die..."* another was sung.

"Baby, I have an idea. Why don't we have a party in memory of Prince. Let's have Dominican do her club all

Purple, play all of Prince's songs and movies, and represent him like it's 1999!"

"YES! That's a great idea," Monte Bucks sat up and said. "I want to invite everybody. Call Jimmy Jam, Morris, call Jay Z, call Lenny Waronker. Let's see if D'Angelo can come and perform. Yes…" Monte Bucks kissed Money. She had found a way to lift his spirits. "Money, what are you waiting for? Call Dominican, tell her my people are coming over there to do her club in all purple!"

"I'm on it," Money said going through her call log for Dominican Flames' number. She smiled, happy that she could bring joy back into Monte Bucks' heart as well as hers.

***

Back in Pittsburgh, things weren't as joyous for Blocks N Bricks. His home had been raided earlier that morning, and he had been served an indictment. Now he was sitting in a cold cell in Federal holding, waiting to make his first appearance.

"Ain't this you?" One of the Federal Agents asked showing him a picture of him and Rick Ross posing at the Teaser Party in the *Hip Hop Weekly* LTMP Special Edition.

Blocks N Bricks looked at himself, but didn't say a word to the Federal Agents. In the other cells beside him he could hear some of his homies talking about the indictment, but he just sat back and listened to them. He was not in the mood to talk. As more and more of them came into the holding area, the sicker he felt. "My rap career's over," he thought.

***

That night at Reflection's night club, fans of Prince poured into the doors. Monte Bucks had even called in a big favor from the Mayor of Pittsburgh. He had got a permit and was allowed to set up huge monitors outside of the club, along with huge movie screens to display the movie *Purple Rain* and to play Prince's music all night.

Inside the club was packed with fans, the LTMP cast, and celebrities. Making his way to the V.I.P section, Smack Down was stopped by Ren. "I know you set me up, nigga. I'ma get wit' you. Not tonight, but we gon' deal, nigga." Ren told Smack Down grabbing him by the arm.

"Whatever, nigga! Get the fuck outta here! Ain't nobody set'cha dumb ass up!" Smack Down said pulling away from Ren.

America ran to up to Smack Down and hugged him.

As she did so, Ren and Smack Down's eyes locked, but there was someone keeping her eyes on Smack Down. Money watched the whole ordeal from the DJ booth.

"Everybody let me get your attention," Monte Bucks said speaking into the mic. Everybody in the club listened to what he was about to say. "Dearly beloved, we are gathered here today fo' this thing we call life…" Everybody recited Prince's words with him.

"Prince was a close friend of mine. I met him during my first tour and we remained friends for close to thirty years. I loved him as a brother, and I know everybody in here loved him as well."

"YAAAAY!" The crowd went crazy.

"TONIGHT! WE GONE REPRESENT LIKE IT'S NINETEEN…"

"NINETY-NINE!" The crowd completed his sentence.

"DJ SCHIZO, LET'S REPRESENT, BAY- BE!"

"YAAAAY!!" The crowd went crazy again.

"Prince's guitar let out a mean riff. He wailed a few exotic moans, the piano played a few keys, the beat was melodic, then he started to sing:

Dig if you will the picture,

you and I engaged in ah kiss,

the sweat of the body covers me.,."

Prince's, *When Doves Cry*, played, and everybody inside and outside of the club sung along.

Monte Bucks held Money King's hand, and danced with her as they sung along. Dominican Flames and America danced as Sexy Duvall watched with a smile on her face. Smack Down held up his baller while him and CNN watched Ren and Hooker watch them.

Prince had brought them all together, and for that night all beefs and business were on hold while Blocks N Bricks, and his co-dee's sat in a Federal Correctional Facility in Ohio, being processed.

***

At Bucks Plaza Hotel, 7:46 A.M. Monte Bucks watched CNN as the spoke about his late friend, Prince. The camera crew from the *Today* show had just packed up and exited his boardroom. He waited for the cast members of LTMP to arrive. They were having a mandatory meeting. Monte Bucks wanted to discuss somethings with them and show the rough edit of episode one.

Around 7:51 A.M., the cast members started arriving, American and Sexy Duvall, GQ Dawg, Dominican Flames, Boom Bap, Mr. Frosty Blow, Smack Down and finally, Making Hitz. There were two empty seats left at the table; one was Money King's, she rarely attended the boardroom meetings, and the other was Blocks N Bricks'.

"While we were mourning Prince, and partying last night, Blocks N Bricks and his crew were getting arrested and processed. I put a folder in front of all of you, I want y'all to study the faces of the two individuals pictured in that folder," Monte Bucks said as he watched everyone look at the photos of detectives Burnam and Gordy. When his assistant went to pay them he had the pictures taken. "These two are trying to scrap up Racketeering charges against us. They try'na shut us d on. We can't let that happened. But the way shit's been lately...Murders, drugs, shootings, were headed that way, and they reminded me of that. But I can't let that happen. So if I have to start cutting fingers off to save the hand, I will. Straightened y'all shit up," Monte Bucks said studying his group of cast members. "I'ma do what I can for Blocks. And I'ma do whatever for the rest of our family if any of you are in need. But don't play me. Don't have me involved with no Federal shit. I don't need to do this. I'm doing this for y'all. I'm doing it for the city. So use me, but don't abuse," Monte Bucks said picking up a remote for the TV. "Now, we about to watch the rough edit for episode one of season two. I'm looking for feedback. If we need to tighten shit up let me know. We want our shit the tightest," Monte Bucks told his cast members as he took a seat and pressed play on the remote.

"This Season on LOVE& TRAP MUZIK, PITTSBURGH"

Made in the USA
Middletown, DE
01 October 2024

61754836R00156